DAD IS FAT

DAD IS FAT

JIM GAFFIGAN

**CROWN
ARCHETYPE**
NEW YORK

Published in the United States by Crown Archetype, an imprint of the Crown Publishing Group, a division of Random House, Inc., New York.
www.crownpublishing.com

CROWN ARCHETYPE with colophon is a trademark of Random House, Inc.

Library of Congress Cataloging-in-Publication Data is available upon request.

ISBN 978-0-385-34905-5
eISBN 978-0-385-34906-2

PRINTED IN THE UNITED STATES OF AMERICA

*Photography credits: All photographs are courtesy of the author, except: page 82,
© Mindy Tucker; page 171, © Kai Cheung; page 275, © Corey Melton.
Jacket design by Michael Nagin
Jacket photography © Gabrielle Revere*

10 9 8 7 6 5 4 3 2 1

First Edition

Dedication and Acknowledgment

This book is dedicated to Jeannie.

For me it feels silly and possibly insulting "dedicating" this book to or "acknowledging" Jeannie here. It doesn't do justice to Jeannie's participation in *Dad Is Fat*. This book really was *our* book. Jeannie not only made me a father and a better comedian, she made me an author. Yes, she is a magic Jeannie. If you are a fan of Jeannie, you will hear her voice in this book. For your sake, I removed all of the yelling. The image of Jeannie sitting at her computer turning my insane drivel into coherent essays while breastfeeding newborn Patrick will stay with me forever. I don't know how I got so lucky to have Jeannie as a writing partner, lover, and friend, but I scored big. She really has ended up being a fantastic first wife.

Contents

Foreword

Jim Gaffigan wrote a book? Isn't he the Hot Pocket guy? I bet he regrets doing that joke. Hooooot Poooockets! I guess that's funny to some people. Why would he write a book? Why would they let him write a book? He doesn't even seem like he's read *a book before. Well, maybe a cookbook. Actually, he seems too lazy to cook. Maybe an eating book. I guess they let anyone write books now. That is if HE actually wrote this book. He probably just talked to some ghostwriter and they turned it into something readable. He looks like a ghost. Is he really that pale? I don't know what's going on with the cover and title.* Dad Is Fat? *I mean, obviously he's fat. Wait, is this the guy with like ten kids? Either way it's just weird to have so many kids today. I hope this isn't one of those complain-about-your-kids books or, even worse, one of those sappy "I love my kids" books. Ugh. Funny, I never say "ugh." Oh, I see what he's doing. He's talking for me, the reader. That's why it's italicized. I certainly wouldn't do that in the foreword of a book.*

Letter to My Children

Dear Children,

I am your dad. The father of all five of you pale creatures. Given how attractive and fertile your mother is, there may be more of you by the time you read this book. If you are reading this, I am probably dead. I would assume this because I can honestly foresee no other situation where you'd be interested in anything I've done. Right now, you are actually more interested in preventing me from doing things like working, sleeping, and smiling. I'm kidding, of course. Kind of. I love you with all of my heart, but you are probably the reason I'm dead.

All right, you didn't kill me. Your mother did. She kept getting pregnant! I don't know how. Don't think about it. It will give you the willies. At one point, I was afraid she got pregnant while she was pregnant. She was so fertile I didn't even let her hold avocados. Anyway, this is a book all about what I observed being your dad when you were very young and I had some hair back in good old 2013.

So why a book? Well, since you've come into my life, you've been a constant source of entertainment while simultaneously driving me insane. I felt I had to write down my observations about you in a book. And also for money, so you could eat and continue to break things. By the way, I'm sorry I yelled so much and did that loud clapping thing with my hands. I hated when my dad would do the loud clapping thing with his hands, so every time I do the loud clapping thing, it pains me in many ways. Most of the pain is because that loud clapping thing actually hurts my hands.

You may be wondering how I wrote this book. From a very early age, you all instinctively knew I wasn't that bright of a guy. Probably from all the times you had to correct me when I couldn't read all the words in *The Cat in the Hat*. Hell, I find writing e-mails a chore. (Thank you, spell-check!) I wrote this book with the help of many people, but mostly your mother. Your mother is not only the only woman I've ever loved, but also the funniest person I know. When your mom was not in labor yelling at me, she made me laugh so hard.

Love,
Dad

P.S. How did you get that hula hoop into that restaurant Easter 2011?

Who's Who in the Cast

Jim Gaffigan (*Dad*). Jim feels honored to be playing the title role of *Dad*. Prior to being cast in *Dad Is Fat*, Mr. Gaffigan also had the title role in the long-running show *Mediocre Uncle*. He is thrilled to be given this opportunity to work with the fine cast of *Dad Is Fat*. "He has virtually no training, skills, or instincts on how to play this role." —*New York Times*

Jeannie Noth Gaffigan (*Mom, Director, Producer, Costume, Hair & Makeup Design, Casting Director, Technical Director, Catering, Music & Lyrics, Usher, Choreographer, Additional Music & Lyrics*). Ms. Noth Gaffigan also coaches Jim Gaffigan in the role of *Dad*.

Marre Gaffigan (*Oldest, Ensemble, Founding Member of the* Dad Is Fat *Company*). Miss Gaffigan is an eight-year-old third grader and an amazing dancer. Off-Broadway: *I Once Had My Own Bed*.

Jack Gaffigan (*First Son, Ensemble, Sound Design & Special Effects*). Jack was last seen in *Yelling for No Reason at All*. He is six and would like to thank God for his incredible good looks, which earned him the leading role in the hit show *I'm Too Cute to Punish*.

Katie Gaffigan (*Middle Child, Ensemble*). Katie is three years old and was the inspiration for the song "You Are My Sunshine." She would like to thank the creators of *Scooby-Doo* and the color green.

Michael Gaffigan (*Gateway Baby, Ensemble*). Michael is one year old and has been dazzling audiences since his 2011 debut. He would like to thank everyone who encouraged him to pursue his childhood dream of playing with a ball.

Patrick Gaffigan (*Newborn, Ensemble*). Patrick is the newest cast member. A truly tireless performer, he has been with the company for only weeks but has already won the award for *Most Colicky Newborn* (2012).

Setting: Present day. A tiny, crowded two-bedroom apartment on the Bowery in downtown Manhattan.

There will be no intermission. Ever.

Rue the Day

When I was single, I was convinced my friends who took the plunge and had their first baby were victims of an alien abduction, because they would disappear from the planet and reappear a year later as unrecognizable strangers. Of course, that may have been because I was way too into *The X-Files.*

When I initially started dating Jeannie, the notion of settling down and having children became a feasible reality for me. Coincidentally, I was invited to visit one of my close childhood friends who had been abducted by aliens—I mean, who got married and had a kid—about a year earlier.

My friend, his wife, and their one-year-old baby had settled in the Southwest. I was working in LA, so a weekend visit was totally doable. I thought it would be great if I brought Jeannie. We could see what it would be like when we got married and had a baby.

My friend Tom (name changed to protect his identity and

possibly preserve the friendship) suggested that we could drive out and hike the Grand Canyon, which to me sounded unnecessarily difficult and way too outdoorsy, but I knew active Jeannie would love it.

Jeannie and I arrived at night. We were much later than expected, due to a flight delay. As we entered Tom's darkened house, we were instructed to please be quiet so as not to wake the baby. I felt like a teenager sneaking back into my parents' house after a missed curfew. We silently tiptoed into a guest room, giggling. "I feel like we're in trouble!" Jeannie whispered. Once we settled in the room, Tom came in and said good night, announcing that we would be leaving around 7 a.m. for the Grand Canyon, so he wanted to get a good night's sleep. As Tom shut the door, Jeannie looked at me confused and said, "I thought you said we would have dinner or something." I looked at my watch: it was 9 p.m. I thought, "Well, he is a parent. I guess this is what parenting involves. This must be what grown-ups do. They skip their second dinner."

The next morning, at the crack of 7 a.m., we set off to make the long, scenic drive to the Grand Canyon. Tom's Saab was seated with men in front and the ladies in back, with the one-year-old in the car seat between them. I suppose the first really big red flag of the trip was the fact that there was one CD allowed to be played in the car. It was explained to us that this CD was meant to soothe the baby. The volume would be occasionally adjusted based on the baby's needs. Um, okay.

So we drove and drove, talking and listening to songs with lyrics like "Ding-a-ding-dong, ding-a-ding-dong." If you haven't driven through the Southwest, the only thing more awe inspiring than the beauty of the landscape is the absence of people. You can drive for hours and never see another person. Restaurants are scarce, expensive, and provide little selection. When we stopped for an early lunch, I ate my first and hopefully last taco salad, with Fritos as the main ingredient. We drove past a drive-thru beef jerky store. Not just a store that only sells beef jerky, but a *drive-thru* store that only sells beef jerky. I guess the drive-thru makes sense, because if you're eating beef jerky, you're probably so busy that you don't have time to get out of your car to buy beef jerky. At one point I started improvising what the owner of the drive-thru beef jerky store was thinking when he came up with the idea for the store. In a ridiculous voice I said: "Fur all dem folks that are in a rush and ain't got time to park der pick-ups and shop fur some quality jerky . . ." It was kind of funny. At least Jeannie and Tom thought so. Tom's wife, Barb (another name change), politely informed me that the voice I was doing was upsetting the baby. I looked back at the baby, who was sound asleep. I didn't know what to say. I just shut up. We drove the rest of the way to the Grand Canyon in complete silence, listening to the soothing baby CD: "Ding-a-ding-dong, ding-a-ding-dong."

We arrived at the Grand Canyon around 1 p.m. The government runs the Grand Canyon "hotels," so they feel more like army barracks. We were standing in line for our housing assignment when Tom's wife announced that the baby needed to go outside. The baby didn't actually say he needed to go outside, but somehow Barb knew that the baby needed to go outside. Either way, Jeannie and I stayed behind to stand in line. Before escorting Barb, who was escorting the baby who wanted to go outside, Tom told me that our reservation was for two side-by-side rooms and to make sure they confirm the rooms were side-by-side. After waiting for another half hour, I reached the counter and was informed that if we wanted side-by-side rooms, it would be an additional hour-long wait. I said that wouldn't be necessary. We would take rooms in different areas.

As they were handing me the keys (actual keys, I might add), Tom approached: "Are the rooms side-by-side?" I explained that, no, if we wanted that, we would have to wait for another hour. Hearing this, Tom got really agitated. He seemed incredibly disappointed in me and demanded that the lady behind the counter give us side-by-side rooms and that we didn't mind waiting. I minded waiting, but again I kept my mouth shut.

After wasting an hour, we unloaded our stuff in our side-by-side rooms and set off to hike the Grand Canyon. Tom and Barb had lived in the area for a while and were experienced at hiking around the Southwest, so they came prepared. Tom gave us special backpacks filled with water, and the baby was secured in a backpack with a sun guard on Barb's back. I felt like we were smuggling the new Dalai Lama out of Tibet. Gear secured, we were all set, and off we went. Twenty minutes into the hike, the baby squeaked a little. Barb immediately announced, "Well, we have to go back. The baby needs a nap."

For a moment, I thought she was joking, but I then realized something horrific. They thought *we* were going to go back, too. It had taken us longer to get the unnecessary gear on than the time we had "hiked." I looked at Jeannie, who was clearly disappointed that she had traveled so far to visit the Grand Canyon for the first time and the day was about to end. She just looked at me like, "Well, I guess we have to go back." In a rare moment of chivalry, I blurted out, "Well, we're going to go on. This may be our only time to do this. That's cool, right?"

After a pause that took way too long, Barb said, "Of course. We'll just go. C'mon, Tom."

Tom seemed frazzled again and asked, "How long do you think you guys are going to be?"

I looked down at the long, winding path, trying to get a glimpse of the Colorado River miles below. "I don't know, an hour or two?"

"Well, please knock at our door when you get back." Wow. I mean, I'm not that out of shape.

After they left, I realized that Jeannie and I had not had a conversation alone since beginning the trip. "I don't know what's going on," Jeannie said, "but I grew up around a lot of babies, and normally babies will nap wherever they are." Not wanting to gossip about my good friend, I just assumed we were ignorant about how daunting the task of having a one-year-old would be. I gave Tom the benefit of the doubt.

Hiking into the Grand Canyon is not easy, but I did it. Unpaid, I might add. I was disappointed to find out that when we were done hiking, we had to climb back *out* of the Grand Canyon. There was no elevator. Can you believe that? Jeannie loved it. My legs burned, I was really exhausted, but I acted like I loved it.

Upon returning to our hotel room we were surprised to see Barb and Tom sitting outside their room next door. Did they get locked out? A weary Tom explained. "We just got the baby to sleep." I remember thinking, "Is this baby ever awake?"

As I unlocked the door to our room, Barb and Tom followed us in and sat on one of the beds. Tom picked up the remote control and started flipping through the three available chan-nels. I apologized and said I needed to take a nap before dinner. Could they possibly watch TV in their own room?

Tom and Barb seemed shocked. "We can't turn on the TV in our room!" Tom snapped. "The baby is sleeping in there! We were hoping we could hang out and watch TV in your room while the baby napped. We've been waiting for you to get back for two hours."

I was confused. Was this what parenting was about? I explained that my legs really hurt and I was really tired and I needed a nap. Tom, obviously trying to contain his anger, asked if after I was done with my *nap*, I could kindly knock at their door so they could come into our room. Again I apolo-gized, but I was barely able to walk. I had to lie down for an hour or I would be done for the rest of the evening. Barb and Tom stormed out.

"Well, that was awkward," said Jeannie. She went to take a shower and do girl stuff while I fell sound asleep with my shoes on for forty-five minutes.

Upon waking from my *nap*, I lightly knocked on their door, and we gathered to head to dinner at some government caf-eteria. Barb, already in pajamas, didn't want to go. When I asked if we could bring her something, she curtly replied, "I ate my dinner already with the baby. It's fine. Just go without me. That's just the life of a mother. Can I use your bathroom to brush my teeth?" Uh, sure. I wouldn't want your raucous teethbrushing to disturb the baby.

On the walk over, I noticed Tom was being very quiet. When I asked if there was anything wrong, he stopped, looked down, and chuckled. "You won't understand till you're a parent."

"I won't understand what?"

He condescendingly explained, "You will *rue the day* you took that nap."

Rue the day? I've rued a lot of days in my life, but I've never rued about a nap. It dawned on me at that moment that the importance of the adjoining rooms was that the baby needed his *own* room and the other room was actually for the four of us. It was meant to serve as a "break room" from attending to the baby, an escape from the arduous chore of parenting. Again, I apologized but couldn't help but think if the rules had been explained at the beginning of the trip, this situation could have been avoided. It seemed to me that the logical thing would have been to outline this arrangement *before* I had screwed up the "break room" situation. An even more logical thing would have been to get *three* rooms and just admit that the baby needed his own room. I was pretty sure this would have allowed us to escape a whole lot of awkwardness, but then again, I'd never been abducted by aliens.

Tom accepted my apology, and the next day we drove back on the long desert highway. It was a relatively quiet drive except for the CD of baby music. "Ding-a-ding-dong, ding-a-ding-dong." Suddenly out of nowhere, a huge deer ran out in front of the car. Tom swerved to avoid it, but the deer froze like, well, like a deer in the headlights. We slammed into the deer at fifty miles an hour. All of us screamed in shock. The car was totaled. The deer ran off injured into the desert. Aside from the deer, everyone was fine, thank God, especially the baby. He didn't wake up from his nap. "Ding-a-ding-dong, ding-a-ding-dong."

"Drinking the Kool-Aid"

I remember looking at people holding babies on airplanes, thinking, "Weirdo. Why would you do that to yourself?" I didn't get it. I essentially looked at parents like they were in a cult, and, frankly, I was right. Parenting is a cult.

This goes way beyond the sleep deprivation and being poorly dressed. The following are characteristics of a cult from the American Family Foundation. I've provided some clarity with the [brackets].

- The group members [parents] display an excessively zealous, unquestioning commitment to an individual [their child].
- The group members [parents] are preoccupied with bringing in new members.
- The group members [parents] are preoccupied with making money.

- The leadership [child] induces guilt feelings in members [parents] in order to control them.
- Members' [parents'] subservience to the group [children] causes them to cut ties with family and friends, and to give up personal goals and activities that were of interest before joining the group.
- Members [parents] are expected to devote inordinate amounts of time to the group [children].
- Members [parents] are encouraged or required to live [in the suburbs] and/or socialize [playdates] only with other group members [parents].

This may be hysterical or frightening to you, but it's only half true. Yes, on the surface parents seem like brainwashed zombies, but we are not. We are not. We love parenting. We love it. You will love it too. Come join us. Join us. You must join us! Please take this pamphlet and watch this Baby Einstein video. Isn't it great? You will grow to love it. It will give you peace. (Help me, I'm trapped.) JOIN US!

To be fair, the intangible benefits of parenting are hidden beneath this scary facade. When I didn't have kids, I didn't get it, and I shouldn't have. I had never fought in the Vietnam War and had dinner in Paris on the same day. I had no context to understand the casualties or the romance a parent feels on the same day. I never knew the joy of successfully putting a two-year-old down for a nap. Well, I still don't, but that's beside the point. For people without kids, parenting is just weird. It can't be articulated. You have to be in the cult to understand it. Obviously, I'm not trying to push you into anything. Make up your own mind in your own time. But the spaceship *is* coming on Thursday.

Family-Friendly

I am considered a clean comedian. This basically means I rarely curse and don't work blue. I never made an intentional decision to be clean; it just ended up that way. When you are discussing mini-muffins in a stand-up act, it's not really necessary to curse or bring sex into the material. Occasionally a reviewer will describe me as "family-friendly," which always makes me cringe.

As a parent, I know "family-friendly" is really just a synonym for *bad*. Family-friendly restaurants serve horrible food. Family-friendly hotels have the charm of a water park. Really, anything with the word *family* before it is bad. Have you been in a "family restroom"? They always seem like they should be connected to a gas station.

The most frightening aspect of "family-friendly" is that it means other families will be present. Other families will by definition have children, which means more screaming. Children have a tendency to behave as poorly as the most poorly behaved kid in the room. The laws of physics dictate that if there is a kid screaming and running in the hallway of a hotel, all the other children will scream and run in the hallway of the hotel.

Probably the only thing worse than the description "family-friendly" is when something is labeled "kid-friendly." Kid-friendly implies there is no consideration for what an adult might need or want. It's not just subquality. It's horrible. It may as well just be called "adult-unfriendly." Maybe the word to be cautious of is *friendly*. When you think about it, *friendly* does communicate some creepiness. It's usually preceded by the word *too*. If someone gets "too friendly," I'm usually suspicious and certainly don't want to be friends with them. Many times people will describe places as *not* being "kid-friendly." That's enough for me. Whenever I hear that a restaurant is "not kid-friendly," I always think, "That place must be awesome! Let's get a sitter."

Have Children:

THE CONDITION

Having five children has really made me appreciate the more important things in life. Particularly the sublime state of being alone. Of course, now I'm never alone. I have five kids who I love with all my heart. Even the one that gave me the title to this book.

This was written by my former son.

The phrase "I have children" is always present tense. They are always with me. Even when I am by myself, I "have children." When I travel I "have children" who I feel guilty being away from. If I'm in the bathroom enjoying some of Daddy's private time, I "have children" who will knock on the bathroom door. "Daddy, what are you doing in there?" As if I'm being rude. I "have children" like I "have male pattern baldness." It is an incurable condition, and I have it. Symptoms include constant fatigue, inability to sleep, and, of course, extreme sleep disruption.

I have become incredibly paranoid around people without kids because I "have children." I feel like it makes me an outcast to people without kids. I watch the faces of single people in their twenties after I bring up that I have children. I imagine them taking a small step backward as if to avoid contagion, with a look of "Sorry to hear that" on their face. Like I naively volunteered to contract leprosy, forever quarantining myself from the world of having fun by having children.

Of course my fear of being rejected by friends without kids is totally unfounded. I have become a hypochondriac about my condition, probably because of the way I viewed people with children when I was a single guy without children. I always thought if I stood too close to someone with kids, I would accidentally slip onto some conveyor belt, get delivered to the suburbs, and start going to bed at a reasonable hour.

But in actuality, my friends without kids have expressed admiration for my courage in dealing with my ailment: "You're so brave!" "Hang in there!" "You're going to get through this!" There is of course some ribbing from my single friends about my not being able to have fun with them by hanging out in a bar all night. I often hear the "whip" sound when I excuse myself from a late-night revelry session. I'll head home to my own late-night revelry session. I'll still have fun and, like my friends, I'll also wake up feeling like a truck drove over me. So I know I'm not missing anything.

Of course, it's not the type of fun my single friends have. I wouldn't expect them to have *that* kind of fun until they catch the bug and they too have children and discover what having fun really is. And by "having fun," I mean "having children" to make you appreciate the sublime state of being alone. I mean, I think it's sublime. I don't remember. I'm not alone often enough to remember things.

The Lone Ranger

I do remember that when I was single, I was a loner by choice. I ate alone, went to movies alone, and even spent time by myself alone. The thought of a roommate to the single me was absurd. Now I have many roommates. I have an eight-year-old, a six-year-old, a three-year-old, a one-year-old, and I don't think I've even met the other one yet. Hey, there are five of them! Five kids may seem overwhelming to you, but how do you think I feel? Ten years ago, I could barely get a date, and now my apartment is literally crawling with babies. It's like I left some peanut butter out overnight.

Not surprisingly, I never imagined I would get married, let alone have children. I suppose I had a romantic notion of having children someday, but, then again, I also had a romantic notion of being an astronaut, and, honestly, being an astronaut felt like a more realistic expectation. Aside from my physiology, nothing in my childhood, teenage years, or early adulthood indicated to me that I would someday have children. Obviously many, many things indicated I would likely be an astronaut. Well, okay, I drank Tang once.

I was the youngest of six kids. Yes, I came from a big family, but really nothing about being the youngest of six kids prepares you for parenthood. It only prepares you to be parented. I was never a babysitter or a camp counselor. I never had a younger cousin or even a neighbor with younger kids. The closest I ever came to a little kid was when I watched the *The Cosby Show* and Raven-Symoné came to live with the Huxtables for a few seasons.

Nothing about my career choice led me to believe I would get married and have children. Being a comedian is a nomadic, nocturnal existence that goes against the basic normalcy and consistency required of being a healthy participant in society, let alone being a healthy participant in raising a child. There were times in my life when I had one thing to do all day, but I still couldn't get to it. "I gotta go to the post office, but I'd probably have to put on pants. And they're only open till five. Looks like I'm going to have to do that next week." Comedians are generally introspective outsiders who identify more with the misfit toys from *Rudolph the Red-Nosed Reindeer* than any "normal" father portrayed on television.

Most stand-up comedians are well aware that they are not normal. There is nothing normal about going onstage and making strangers laugh. Try it sometime. It's really weird. We are natural contrarians. Tell a comedian to do something and they will most likely do the opposite just to see how you react. "You should play football like your brother"; "You should go into finance like your father"; "You should write an intelligent, funny, and well-crafted book like Bill Cosby."

Just when I was resigned to the reality of a future of being the proud weird uncle who lived in New York City, I met Jeannie. Jeannie was unlike any woman I had ever met or have yet to meet. She was part girl next door, part superstar, part insane-asylum inpatient. Jeannie was the oldest of nine children, and when I met her she was directing a Shakespearean play with a hip-hop score featuring about fifty inner-city kids. For *free*. Here was this funny, sexy, smart woman who was passionate about her art and, for some reason, children. Working with kids inspired Jeannie's creativity, and being with her inspired me. It was an amazing relationship. Jeannie literally wanted to take care of me, and in turn I had this crazy, almost biological desire to provide her with, well, someone to take care of.

For the first time in my life, I felt like I could spend the rest of my life with someone. Heck, I could even have a child with this person. Even if I knew nothing about kids, Jeannie could just handle everything, right? I already knew I wouldn't have to pay her. Eventually I tricked Jeannie into marrying me. It was at that point that I discovered Jeannie is someone who gets pregnant looking at babies.

So now I am a loner with a chronic and acute case of children. I am learning to live with my condition as well as encourage others who have found themselves in a similar state. Therefore I have organized an annual Sleep-a-Thon to help raise money for research. If you would like to sponsor me, and I am sure you do, please pledge $100 for every one hour I sleep. You will be doing a great humanitarian service, and I will be a better father because of your kindness and support. It's a win-win situation. I realize this sounds like you would just be paying me to sleep, but it's more. Together we can make the condition of having children a lot more bearable. Well, more bearable for me and my bank account. Thank you for your generosity.

Bedridden with children.

Anti-Family

I enjoy posting blurbs and observations on Twitter and Facebook about my children and parenting. Mostly I post about how ill-equipped and overwhelmed I am as a parent and how babies for some reason don't like the taste of wasabi. The blurbs are meant to be (hopefully) funny, silly, and/or insightful. Some of these observations will lean toward a dark, sarcastic take on the prison sentence that is parenthood. In a family-friendly way, of course.

Occasionally I receive comments that associate my musings with being anti-family, or somehow dissuading people from having kids. These occasional comments are so absurd they always make me laugh. I wonder if my rant on not wanting to work out is contributing to the obesity epidemic. Maybe I'm also increasing cake sales. I never knew I had so much power.

Anti-family? This could not be further from the truth. I love being a parent and enjoy finding the humor in parenting. If you complain about how you spend your Saturdays taking your kid to birthday parties, that means you are taking your kid to birthday parties. If you complain about how hard it is to get your kid to read, it means you are trying to get your kid to read. If you are complaining about your kid not helping around the house, that means you have a fat, lazy kid. You joke about it. That's how you deal. If parents don't like being a parent, they don't talk about being a parent. They are absent. And probably out having a great time somewhere. I have done extensive research and, almost universally, found that the people who view my blurbs and observations as "anti-family" are dicks. Failing and laughing at your own shortcomings are the hallmarks of a sane parent.

When you are handed your screaming newborn for the first time, you are simultaneously handed a license for gallows humor. The guy who invented the phrase "Don't throw the baby out with the bathwater" probably had a baby. And, for a moment, probably contemplated throwing the baby out.

I Confess

I wasn't ready for the guilt of being a parent. I was raised
Catholic, so guilt is a familiar friend. Guilt is as much a part
of the Catholic culture as is rooting for Notre Dame. I grew
up with a "God is watching you, so you better not make him
mad" mentality. I felt guilty for feeling good, for feeling bad,
and for feeling nothing. Attending Confession was supposed
to alleviate some of the guilt, but I always ended up feeling
guilty for not telling the priest everything I felt guilty about, so
I stopped going to Confession. Then I felt guilty that I stopped
going to Confession. That's a lot of guilt. Just when I thought
that nothing could top "Catholic Guilt," I became acquainted
with "Parental Guilt," which totally puts "Catholic Guilt" to
shame. Sorry, Catholic Guilt. Now I feel guilty for shaming
you. Well, at least now you know how I feel.

No matter how hard you try to be a good parent, you always know deep down that you could do more. I feel guilty

when I travel out of town to do shows. I feel guilty when I'm in town and I don't spend every single moment with my children. I feel guilty when I'm spending time with my children and I am not doing something constructive toward their intellectual development. I feel guilty when I feed them unhealthy food they like. I feel guilty when I feed them healthy food they don't like. I feel guilty when I drop them off at school. I feel guilty when I pick them up at school. I feel guilty mostly for writing this book instead of spending time with them. Great, now I've probably made you feel guilty for reading this book. I feel guilty about that now, too. Sorry. Probably what I feel *most* guilty about is how many times I have used the word *guilty* in this essay. Again, let me sincerely apologize. Wow. I feel so much better after this confession. You were right, Catholic Guilt. Thank you.

Happy Days Are Here Again

I've never really been considered cool. It always felt like an un-attainable goal. Maybe it was my pale skin or pudgy features, but I never looked cool in a leather jacket or a pair of shorts. Even when I was wearing them at the same time. I realized long ago I was never destined to grace the cover of *Rolling Stone.*

This is not to say that cool wasn't important to me as a teen-ager. Growing up, "cool" felt like an assignment that I was always turning in late. I wasn't "un-cool," which in high school means "a walking target of mockery and ridicule," but that was always a looming fear. I still was allowed to hang out with some cool kids because I occasionally said something funny. I remember thinking that one of those cool kids had really "cool" parents. They weren't incredibly wealthy, but his mom and dad showed up at everything looking exceptionally stylish. They threw a Christmas party every year that all the other parents wanted to be invited to. They never seemed frazzled or appeared to get upset about anything. They always had the latest gadgets and went on amazingly stylish vacations. They dressed their kid in the hippest clothes possible. Their kid was "cool" by default, which in high school means "royalty." I remember thinking, "My parents are so un-cool. If they were cool, I too would be cool. If I'm dumb enough to have kids when I grow up I am definitely going to be a 'cool' parent."

Well, guess what? I am a parent now, and I am still not cool. I also see a lot of former cool kids trying to be cool parents, but it's not working. Why? Because parenting is not cool. You know what else isn't cool? Trying to be cool. Sorry, everyone, you're never going to be Gwen Stefani or David Beckham. Hell, they probably aren't even considered cool anymore. Cool is subjective. Were that kid's parents really cool? I bet he didn't think so. Actually, back then, I only remember one kid ever saying to me that his parents were "cool," but what he meant was that they smoked pot with him. Even then, I thought his parents were total degenerates.

Since becoming a dad, I have become painfully aware of the obsession with cool parenting. There are three-year-olds decked out head to toe in designer clothes. I have to assume a few of these three-year-olds didn't pick out their own outfits. Some of them might not even have credit cards. There are magazines, blogs, and websites obsessed with "cool parenting" that recommend the latest thing to feed your child, cool furniture for your child, and cool things to do with your child if you want them to be around children of other cool parents. I understand the aspiration. The fifteen-year-old me really relates. What I find odd is that the people who frequent and post comments on some of these parenting websites seem like some of the un-coolest people in the universe. I used to have a lot of faith in humanity before the advent of the website "comment" section. These brave, anonymous parents shamelessly gossip and snipe at one another, bragging about how smart and cool their kids are and mocking people who don't share their "cool" opinions. Newsflash: High school is over. You are not cool. "Cool" is a ridiculous concept.

I find it hysterical that "ironic" is currently considered "cool" when, in fact, "cool" itself is what is ironic. Even in the '70s and '80s, the television show *Happy Days* was aware of the irony of "cool." The cool character on *Happy Days* was "the Fonz," and he was ridiculous. His office was in a men's bathroom. That's not only not cool, that's not even sanitary. Maybe our society's confusion about "cool" actually originates from *Happy Days*. Most of us watched it when we were too young to understand sarcasm. We all actually thought that "the Fonz" was the coolest guy in the world because that's what the TV told us. That guy who can hit a jukebox and make it play or snap his fingers and have two chicks at his side is cool! I want to be like that guy. The guy with the greasy hair who hangs out by a urinal.

To the Fonz's credit, "cool" originated as a term meant to describe someone who ignores the conventions of the social mainstream. They just don't care what other people think and do their own thing. Now everyone is looking to blogs and media outlets to find out what's cool? If you are looking to see what everyone else is doing to try to be cool, you are probably not cool.

As if journalists know anything about being cool. In high school, if you wanted to find out what was cool, the last people you would ask would be the kids that worked on the high school newspaper: "Hey, guys, can you tell me somewhere cool to go this weekend? You know, someplace where you guys are not going to be?" I know this is true, because I worked on the school newspaper.

It is also ironic that in high school, the jocks were cool and the nerds were not cool. Now the nerds are the tastemakers. The nerds are rich and successful, and those jocks are dumb divorced guys with beer bellies. By the way, in high school, I also played football and, yes, I have a beer belly. Jeannie can't divorce me. We are Catholic. Thank you, Jesus.

So parents who want to be considered cool, give it up. Even if you put your three-year-old in a fedora, we all know you are still getting barfed on and wiping noses and butts like the rest of us. No matter how cool you try to be, we all know you are spending more time in the bathroom than the Fonz. "Ayyy!"

The Pharaoh and the Slave

When I was growing up, I always assumed my father had six children so he could have a sufficient lawn crew. Every Saturday, my dad would have me and all my siblings out doing yard work, landscaping and what seemed like arbitrarily excavating our yard. He would say things like "Today I'd like to move this hill." At best, it felt like torture. At worst, it felt like slavery. I remember thinking that dads were the ultimate bosses. All-powerful. In charge of everything. The father was the pharaoh, and we were the slaves building his pyramids. I had no idea at the time that I was not the slave, but actually the master. My father was the slave. Okay, maybe not the slave, but he was certainly not the master.

Now that I am a father myself, I know that powerlessness is the defining characteristic of fatherhood. This begins with the pregnancy. Men spend their whole lives being active. We evolved as hunters. "Me get job, me get girl, me get girl pregnant. Now me shut mouth and wait for girl to tell me what to do." As expectant fathers, we become silent spectators. Passive participants in a series of external events over which we have zero control.

Sure, you help when you can. You rub shea butter on your partner's belly. You eat like you are pregnant. You buy those tiny diapers that are the size of an iPhone and that will only fit the baby for three days. You eat some more. You attend those bogus birthing classes and learn support techniques that you forget the second you're out the door, because you have to get something to eat. Really, you don't know what you are doing or what you should be doing, so you mostly try to stay out of the way and eat. Well, that's what I did.

While your baby is being born, you witness the most amazing thing that will happen in your life, but you're not physically participating. During the delivery, you feel like one of those NASA engineers sitting in front of some panel of switches and buttons watching the space shuttle take off. This is your baby, but today you are just the engineer in a short-sleeve dress shirt with a pocket protector and 1970s government-issued glasses helplessly watching the defining moment of the thing that you helped create. Doing the countdown but not launching the rocket.

During labor, the father-to-be is always attempting to justify his presence in the room: "Hey, I'm the dad. I'm on the team. I caused this. Well, I'm in the way, so I will just stand here in the corner and take some pictures."

You want to be there for emotional support, yet everything you say or do ends up irritating the mother-to-be while she is in labor. WARNING: Labor is not the time to try out new jokes on her or eat chips and guacamole with extra garlic. I don't understand why she wouldn't want one bite. Anytime is a good time for guacamole, right?

The tradition of letting the father "cut the cord" is such an obvious attempt to fabricate a reason for the father to even be there: "Let's find something for this incompetent boob to do." They present the duty of cutting the cord as if it's a magic bonding ceremony. In reality, you're just the dorky guy snipping the ribbon in front of a new building that you didn't build. It's ironic that the man whose virility caused this whole situation is now the most impotent person in the room.

The umbilical cord is the conduit of life for the unborn baby. It is connected to the placenta, which is the entire source of food and oxygen for the unborn child. When baby takes his first breath, there is no longer any reason for him to be connected to the cord. Who better than the father to be the one to release his child from the life source of the womb and transition him to the outer world? After all, you are the one that's going to push them out of the house when they turn thirty. You are handed the scissors and given the job of trying to saw through the slimy human USB cord without screwing something up. And, by the way, you can't screw it up. They wouldn't give you that much responsibility. The cord is clamped already, so it's not even a medical procedure. It's a symbol. "Now you will symbolically release the child from the mother's care . . . and then immediately return him to his mother's care for the next thirty years."

After the delivery, you end up being the overzealous security guard who originally wanted to be a cop: "Oh, you want to see the mother and new baby? Let me see some ID. Did you wash your hands?" You pretend you're in charge, but you mostly feel completely powerless. You'll feebly watch the baby and mother of your child lie there recovering, knowing that anything you do that is not mom or baby related may be viewed as insulting. Should I get her food? A blanket? Would that be overbearing? Should I get *me* food? A blanket? Would that be selfish? I guess I'll just stare. Men used to pass out cigars in the waiting room. Now we just stand there feeling about as useful as a cigar in a hospital waiting room. We accept the congratulations from friends and return to our security guard post unaware that we've just been appointed Vice President.

Vice President

As a dad, you are Vice President. You are part of the Executive Branch of the family, but you are the partner with the weaker authority. In your children's eyes, you mostly fulfill a ceremonial role of attending pageants and ordering pizza.

I'm never the first choice. My kids don't even mask it, which I respect them for. "Let's see, the crabby guy with the scratchy beard or that warm soft lady that tells us stories for eight hours?" It's not even close.

Jeannie is Bill Clinton, and I am Al Gore. She "feels their pain," and I'm the dork reminding them to turn off the lights. I'm always Joe Biden saying the wrong thing. When I read a story to my children, I know how Dan Quayle felt when he spelled *potato* wrong. Most dads know they are Vice Presidents and are fine with it. Being "President Mom" is a position outside of our pay grade or skill set. We can't breastfeed, and we wouldn't know how to braid hair anyway.

Other times, we dads are presented as the "enforcer" Vice President, the Dick Cheney. "If you don't listen to me, I'm going to tell your father." Suddenly the lame-duck dad is Darth Vader. I don't know how kids keep it straight. They must think, "So if we don't behave, you'll report our behavior to that guy you yell at and boss around the house? Well, that's not threatening at all."

Most of the time, I don't even care about the crimes my children have supposedly committed while under my wife's watch. However, I'll still put on the stern-father face. "Your mother told me you were climbing on furniture and when she asked you to stop, you didn't listen to her. Is that true?" My children will "act" apologetic and frightened, but it feels false because, in reality, my children don't fear me the way I feared my father. When I have discipline talks with my children, it almost seems like we are shooting a scene from *Growing Pains*.

Occasionally, decisions are gratuitously placed in the "Ask Your Dad" category, under the pretense that your opinion is valued, but you know better than to go against your President. "Yes, sure. Why not? It's absolutely fine with me . . . unless your mom didn't want me to say that . . . in that case, absolutely no! I forbid it." That's when you realize you not only have no idea what you are doing, you also have no principles. You have become the "God help us if something happens to the President" Vice President.

My Dad, the Professional Wrestler

When I first became a father, I remember thinking that my ultimate goal was to just not make the same mistakes that my father made. Then I was comforted by the thought that there was no way I would be able to afford all that booze. My father may not have been the best dad, but without the comparison to him, I would probably feel even guiltier, so in a way he made me a better dad.

Not too many dads of my father's generation were great dads. Truth be told, my dad probably tried his best. He was a good provider. It wasn't like any other dads were reading stories or picking up kids from school either. My dad was of a pre–Phil Donahue time. Back in the '70s, aside from putting food on the table, most dads essentially did nothing to raise their kids. I should also mention that in my dad's era, "putting food on the table" never actually involved *putting* food *on* the table. That was women's work. Dads didn't *put* food on the table. They didn't *put* a diaper on a baby, and they didn't *put* a kid in a bath. They also didn't actually *"bring home the bacon."* Nor did they shop for the bacon or cook the bacon. They just ate the bacon. Who wouldn't? Bacon is delicious. The amazing thing is not that they didn't do any of these things, it's that they didn't feel guilty about it at all. I have my own baby sling, and I still feel guilty all the time.

Smiling through the guilt.

I'm told many young children view their dad as a superhero. Someone brave and strong who will protect them from bad guys and is able to leap tall buildings in a single bound. Not me. I will always remember my dad in the mythical proportions normally reserved for professional wrestlers. Like those cartoonish champions of the ring, all my dad's habits and mannerisms seemed exaggerated for my amazement, entertainment, and frustration. He'd enter the room with a cloud of intimidation that rivaled André the Giant stepping onto the canvas. To this day, an abrupt silencing cough scares the hell out of me. I feared him. His temper. My father's size was not overwhelming, but his presence was enormous. He could shake a room with a never-ending pause. He could cut my knees out with his evil eye. I could feel the vibrations from him walking on those heavy heels, smell his cigarette in the air, and suddenly fear would fill my stomach. My siblings feared my dad. *Everyone* feared my dad. I remember my one friend deciding if he should come over based on whether or not my father was home. My dad once shot a man for snoring! Okay, he didn't, but to the sixteen-year-old me, he was the type of person who would have if he lived in the Wild West and had a gun and someone was snoring or breathing near him.

My dad was not mean. He was controlling and demanding. He wouldn't take no for an answer. He was not above enlisting my friends into the family yard work detail. He certainly did not tolerate moping.

DAD: [*Cough.*] Get out there and be in a good mood.
ME: But, Dad, it's a funeral.
DAD: [*Cough.*] I don't care. Now go stand near the casket. I
     want to get some pictures.

My father never really understood technology. As an adult, if I wasn't home when he called, he would leave the same message on my answering machine.

> DAD: [*Beeeeep.*] [*Cough.*] Hello. Hello? Hello! [*Long pause.*] Tell Jim his dad called!

I always wanted to call him back and say, "Yeah, Dad, my answering machine told me you called. Then the toaster told me I was hungry."

The fatigue of being the father of six set in by the time I was a teenager. The night before I went to college, my dad sat me down.

> DAD: [*Cough.*] Now, Jim, I'm not sending you to college so you can get drunk and flunk out.
>
> ME: Well, then I'm not going. You're going to have to send a neighbor.

Of course, that's not what I said. That is what I thought, but I didn't want to get verbally body slammed. My dad could be warm and generous, but he always seemed to be treating people to things they didn't necessarily want: "[*Cough.*] Tomorrow we are going to get up at five a.m. and sit on a boat for twelve hours in the blistering heat until your head turns a bright beet-red. Happy birthday!"

Every year for our birthday, our dad would take us out to dinner. We could pick any restaurant in town, and he would take us there. Any restaurant at all, as long as it was Giovanni's, my father's favorite restaurant. Every year, it seemed like the same conversation.

> DAD: [*Cough.*] This year for your birthday, your mother and I want to take you out to dinner. Just the three of us. Where would you like to go?
> ME: Thanks. I was thinking House of Kobe.
> DAD: You don't want to go to Giovanni's?
> ME: We went there last year. We always go there. How about House of Kobe?
> DAD: I think your mother wants to go to Giovanni's.
> ME: Well, it's my birthday. I'd like to go to House of Kobe, if that's okay.
> DAD: Fine. [*Cough.*] We'll go to House of Kobe.

Hours later, we would be in the car, my parents seated in the front, with me in the back. My dad would look at me in the rearview mirror.

> DAD: You wanted to go to Giovanni's, right?
> ME: Uh, sure.

I would get frustrated and occasionally challenge my dad, but I always lived in fear. I remember my mother telling me, "You're never going to change him." To my mother and siblings, challenging my father was a pointless, losing battle. Why kick the hornet's nest? Why risk getting him mad? After all, he would shoot a man for snoring.

My mother and father died many years ago. Thanks for

bringing it up. Time has turned my mother into something of a saint in my memory. Mostly because she stayed married to my dad. Actually she really was an amazing mother. Time has also softened my view of my father, but somehow I still fear him. The clink of ice in a glass or the smell of cigarettes still makes me stand a little straighter.

My dad, my brothers, and I out celebrating
after my dad shot a man for snoring.

It's actually unfair to characterize my father, or anyone for that matter, by only their dark side. I certainly wouldn't want to be described by only the stupid and buffoonish things I've done. I'm sure I have my own Giovanni's. As a teenager,

I did view my father as this brutish, selfish, controlling Hulk Hogan, but now I see a bigger picture. My dad was a strict but compassionate man who cared deeply about his family, co-workers, and community. My dad never left my mother's side for an entire year as she lost her battle with ovarian cancer. I loved my father. Most people did. He did try his best. He did provide for his family. He taught me many things and gave me a work ethic that made me who I am today: a guy who would throw his own father under the bus in a book about parenting.

I'm probably a comedian because of my father. I loved making my mother laugh, but the impression of my father I did for my siblings changed the trajectory of my life. When I lampooned the feared dictator of our lives, I had my sisters' and brothers' attention and respect. For a moment I wasn't simply the youngest or just another competitor for food. I was an equal. It was very empowering. I liked the feeling.

By today's standards, my dad wouldn't be considered the greatest dad, and I'm sure his dad wouldn't be considered the greatest dad either. I'm sure my grandfather's dad would be considered an even worse dad. It probably goes all the way back to cavemen fathers just eating their children. What I'm trying to say is, dads are getting better. Either that or we are all slowly being turned into women. At least that's what my gynecologist thinks.

The Narcissist's Guide to Babies and Toddlers

Getting married and becoming the father of young children has taught me that I am a narcissist. The good news is that I am a really great, really important, and really special narcissist. I lived my life as a single man, and even for a few years into parenthood, just looking out for number one. If I picked up my mail, went in my apartment, and saw there was a letter for a neighbor, I'd think, "Looks like they're never getting this. It would take way too much energy to go back outside. Besides, right now I have to watch some *Wheel of Fortune.*"

My perceived needs were all-important. When it came to my career, relationship, or taking the last piece of pizza, I was only thinking about myself. And, of course, the pizza. My stand-up act was established on a lazy, gluttonous, selfish point of view and, based on my success, people identified. Turns out everyone is a closet narcissist. Except you, of course. You're perfect. Keep reading.

Unfortunately, these narcissistic traits that made me a popular comedian do not work well for someone who truly desires to be a good husband or parent. I'm not saying parenting cured my narcissism, but it changed me and continues to change me every day. I am now a teeny tiny bit less of a narcissist. Being a parent is a selfless adventure. The worldview of "Take care of yourself first" is no longer logical to a sane person if your baby wakes up hungry in the middle of the night. You can't be like, "What's that? The baby is starving? Eh, forget her, I've got to get some sleep." For me, parenting was literally a wake-up call from my own simple selfishness. In other words, I'm not *quite* as horrible as I used to be. Raising kids may be a thankless job with ridiculous hours, but at least the pay sucks.

One would think it would be impossible to raise a child and remain a narcissist. That is completely untrue, and I am living proof. There are even some people whose narcissism is what motivates them to have children. This is an easy trap to fall into. We all harbor a secret desire to produce a child that is an extension of ourselves . . . especially me, because most bald, pudgy, newborn babies look exactly like me, but a little less adorable.

Of course, babies and toddlers are all narcissists. But they are *supposed* to believe the whole world revolves around them. It's part of their natural development and a bunch of other stuff Freud said that I am too dumb to explain. One thing I do know: it doesn't work to have two narcissists competing against each other in a parent/child relationship. If you don't believe me, just try to convince a three-year-old to give you the last cookie. There is a lot of screaming and crying, and the kid gets a little upset, too. It's a daily struggle.

So now that I've admitted that I'm a narcissist, I'd also like to admit that I'm probably not the greatest parent. The last thing I want is one of my kids reading this book in ten years and thinking, "That guy thought he was a good parent?" I don't know why my children would refer to me as "that guy," but I'm keeping my expectations low. I'm probably not the best parent, but I am trying. I'll complain and joke about parenting and kids, but every parent knows it's a heroic endeavor, and we participants need to laugh at it. After all, suicide is off the table now.

When Women Get Lazy

I am undeniably lucky to have married a woman like Jeannie. She is energetic, hardworking, and takes incredible care of the kids and me. However, during our marriage there have been periods when she has become rather lazy. Jeannie describes these periods as "pregnancy." My view has always been, pregnant or not, that does not mean she can't move some cinder blocks. We are a team, and I have to take a second nap today.

Of course, pregnant women are not lazy. In fact, they are the opposite of lazy. Whatever they are doing, they are also always growing a baby. Even when they are sleeping, they are growing a baby. They are constantly multitasking. I'm often not even tasking.

This is because women are amazing. And I mean that in a very pandering way. (I've been told more women than men buy and read books, so there is your shout-out, ladies.) But truly, women are amazing. Think about it this way: a woman can grow a baby inside her body. Then a woman can deliver the baby through her body. Then, by some miracle, a woman can feed a baby with her body. When you compare that to the male's contribution to life, it's kind of embarrassing, really. The father is always like, "Hey, I helped, too. For like five seconds. Doing the one thing I think about twenty-four hours a day. Well, enjoy your morning sickness—I'm going to eat this chili. Mmmm, smell those onions." You can't eat chili in front of a pregnant woman. Sometimes you can't cough, snore, or breathe around a pregnant woman. Most important, you can't complain around a pregnant woman. I know that because I've lived with one for eight years. Every one of the man's problems is insignificant on a relative basis.

HUSBAND: I'm tired.
PREGNANT WOMAN: Oh, really? I'm growing a human being.
HUSBAND: I have so much work to do.
PREGNANT WOMAN: Oh, really? I have to push a baby with your head size out of my body.
HUSBAND: I'm going to stand in the corner for the next nine months.

Witnessing Jeannie give birth to five healthy babies has taught me many things, but mostly that I could never have a baby. Granted, I don't have a uterus. But even if I did have a uterus, I don't think I could do any of it. If men had the baby, our species would be long extinct. That's why females always have the babies. Except in the seahorse world: supposedly the male seahorse has the baby. I don't understand why they didn't just call that the female seahorse. It was probably some stubborn scientist's fault.

> STUBBORN SCIENTIST: [*Condescending.*] And that one there is the male seahorse.
> STUBBORN SCIENTIST'S ASSISTANT: Um, Bill, sorry to interrupt, but that seahorse is having a baby.
> STUBBORN SCIENTIST: Oh . . . [*Beat.*] . . . the *male* seahorse has the baby. You're fired.

Pregnancy is an incredible sacrifice. I used to think morning sickness should be used to describe us people sick of getting up in the morning, but morning sickness is no joke. It's incredible what a woman's body goes through when she's growing a baby. I can barely digest cheese, and Jeannie has endured five full-term pregnancies. Suddenly, simple actions like eating, sleeping, peeing, and tying shoes become Olympic hurdles. I only remember Jeannie complaining once or twice: "I'm tired. I'm hungry. I'm cold. Let me back inside." Being a supportive spouse, I would explain that I'd let her back in the house once she moved those cinder blocks. A deal is a deal.

During pregnancy, the dominant hormone is progesterone, which is a Latin term for *shut up and get away from me, you horrible man who ruined my life.* By the way, here is a piece of advice for you soon-to-be-fathers out there: pregnant women don't like to be called "bitches" AT ALL. You're welcome.

I'm jealous of pregnant women. When pregnant women have cravings, it's "adorable" and when they put on twenty or thirty pounds in nine months, it's "healthy." Yet when I have cravings and put on thirty pounds, I'm considered a "fat tub of turds." I'm not sure, but I believe this is sexism. Everyone wants to rub a pregnant women's belly, but when I ask people to rub *my* belly, I get kicked out of Dave & Buster's. It's just not fair. I put on more weight than Jeannie during each of her pregnancies. I justify it by thinking, "Well, just another thing I'm better at than she is."

Still half the size of my stomach.

Oh My God, You're Pregnant?

Pregnancy is an abstract concept to grasp. You see the baby bump, and people are congratulating you and your wife, but you really don't know what's going on in there until you see that 3-D ultrasound. Very early on, you can see a fully formed baby who is kicking and sucking its thumb. I remember being shocked when I first saw my son on a twelve-week ultrasound. He already had more hair than I did.

It can be confusing deciphering our society's view toward pregnancy. Culturally, we cherish a pregnant woman. We acknowledge the sacrifice. People will give up their seats on buses. We say "Congratulations" when we see a pregnant woman, but there is usually an element of scandal associated with it. Pregnant women are either too young or too old, or it's too soon after another pregnancy, or she's going to get in trouble at work. She's too poor, too rich, too successful, too skinny, too fat, too crazy, too busy, too single, too married, too too.

"Oh my God! Your sister is pregnant? She was just a *kid* twenty years ago!" Why are we always surprised to find out someone is pregnant? Really, *getting* pregnant is the most amazing unamazing thing ever. Of course conception is miraculous, but it *is* how we all got here. My mom got pregnant. Your mom got pregnant. EVERYONE'S mom got pregnant. Yet still we're shocked it could happen to any other woman. We are shocked when a teenager gets pregnant. We're shocked when a fifty-year-old gets pregnant. But, really, that's how it's been happening forever. As human beings, we end up acting like we are the first generation on this planet to deal with pregnancy. We are most shocked when really attractive, successful women get pregnant. It's unbelievable. "Did you hear Beyoncé got pregnant? It's almost as if she's a human being!" There's always that unspoken commentary of "Why would she do that to her career?" How many Grammy Awards would Beyoncé need to win before it would be time for her to have a baby?

I think there may be a belief mothers are no longer sexy or somehow an exception if they are sexy. The concept of a MILF is rather insulting if it's based on the belief that having a baby makes you unattractive. So, therefore, the rare mother who *is* attractive needs her own special term. Actually "MILF" is pretty insulting anyway. Sorry I brought it up, ladies. I think Jeannie gets sexier with every baby she has. And I'm not just saying that because she will most likely be reading this book. Hi, Jeannie. Sorry I destroyed the microwave last night, again. Can you clean it up? Think about it, though: When you see a gorgeous woman, and then you find out she's had a bunch of kids, doesn't it make her like a hundred times hotter?

It's not just celebrity moms. We are surprised that *any* beautiful, successful woman would want to have a baby. Why would she want to do that? I don't know. Why would your mom want to have you? As if without the ticking of some socially imposed biological clock, no women would voluntarily choose to get pregnant. People treat having a kid as somehow retiring from success. Quitting. Have you seen a baby? They're pretty cute. Loving them is pretty easy. Smiling babies should actually be categorized by the pharmaceutical industry as a powerful antidepressant. Being happy is really the definition of success, isn't it?

Witchcraft

Jeannie has had all our babies at home in our apartment. Hey, we've got the room, right? If you are unfamiliar with home birth, like I was, you probably think of it as taking a hundred years of advancement in the field of obstetrics and just throwing that away. You just wing it. Well, that's what I thought, too. During the birth of our first child, I remember thinking, "Hey, I can't program a DVR, but I'm here to help. Now where would you like me to stand terrified? That will be my contribution."

At times, it seems we elected to have our babies at home mostly to make other people feel uncomfortable. I quickly learned that people don't want to hear about home births. Their first reaction always seems to be, "Oh, you had your baby at home. Yeah, we were going to do that, too, but we wanted our baby to live." There's usually an assumption of irresponsibility or laziness: "You didn't want to go to the hospital?" I sometimes explain that the hospital was, like, twenty blocks away and that I didn't feel like putting on pants. "Weren't you worried that something would go wrong?" Don't most people worry at the hospital? Hospitals should just be renamed "houses of worry." Actually, we had our babies at home, not in a Waffle House. "At home? Isn't that a little too comfortable? Why didn't you have the baby in that germ-infested building where sick people congregate? Didn't your wife want to give birth in a gown someone died in yesterday?"

Believe me, I get the concern. Home birth sounds crazy. It is a wild experience. I remember at our last home birth, there was so much screaming at one point, I actually woke up. I thought someone had scored a touchdown or something. When I saw my wife was just having another baby, I asked her to keep it down and went back to sleep.

It may come as no surprise that home birth was Jeannie's idea. I'm not really even a fan of cooking at home. At all of our home births, I was Jeannie's birth coach, which is a generous title for "that guy in the way." In reality, I would assist by performing counterpressure and get yelled at for doing it wrong. Don't worry, it wasn't just Jeannie and me; there was a midwife there, which means we believe in witchcraft. Actually, a midwife is a certified medical practitioner. She is *not* your "extra wife" and will not make you breakfast. I learned this the hard way. Most midwives are actually former labor and delivery nurses, which means that they have more experience with the whole labor from beginning to end than some doctors do. With healthy labors, doctors come in the bottom of the ninth and catch the ball for the winning last out, whereas midwives have been in for the whole game.

Jeannie's first home birth was not even originally planned to be a home birth. The birth was supposed to be "natural," without drugs in a birthing center at the hospital. It was to be at Bellevue Hospital, which I've always thought of as a mental hospital. Given how crazy Jeannie and I are, I thought it was only appropriate that she give birth in a hospital that was famous for its mental ward.

During the first and second trimester of her pregnancy, I remember nodding along to Jeannie's excited tutorial as she explained all she had learned about natural childbirth versus C-section, the Bradley Method, and home birth. Like most of you reading this, I would end every discussion with "Well, obviously we're not having the baby in our apartment, right?" Jeannie would assure me "No," and then I would go back to whatever I was eating. Our "birth plan" was to wait until Jeannie was far enough into labor that she could have the baby naturally at the hospital in a birthing center without medical intervention or drugs. Great. As the pregnancy got into its third trimester, Jeannie became more and more enamored with home birth. She began talking about having our next baby at home. Great, whatever, and I went back to whatever I was eating. When she finally went into labor with Marre, we still were planning on going to Bellevue. The midwife came over, monitored the baby, and Jeannie walked around the apartment distressing about eventually going to the hospital.

By this time, I was aware that home birth was a safe alternative, but I still expected to be heading to the hospital at any moment. We had a bag packed and everything. The baby was in the right position, healthy with a strong heartbeat, and Jeannie just needed regular contractions to push the baby out.

Then I remember Jeannie turning to me and announcing she wanted to have the baby at home. She was way too uncomfortable to go anywhere. Um, great. I stopped eating. I didn't know what to do.

The midwife had all the necessary medical items for a home birth with her and told me to warm some towels and cover the things that we didn't want blood on. Um, okay. "Blood on"? I'd never attended a birth, let alone a home birth. So I went to work. When the midwife and Jeannie eventually returned from the bathroom to the living room, they started laughing. Well, Jeannie was making pain noises, but there were some laughterlike sounds in her pain noises.

I had put a shower curtain on the floor, covered the couches and our new flat-screen TV with garbage bags. The midwife asked, "What do you think is going to happen in here?" I never said I was smart.

The labor was long and painful for Jeannie, but she did it. Marre arrived as we were all kneeling on the living room floor. The baby was perfect and healthy, and we were at home. I was so impressed by the midwife. She was incredibly skillful and professional but at the same time peaceful and respectful during the process. We all celebrated with champagne, and Jeannie and I got to sleep in our own bed. We were convinced. If we were going to have more babies and the pregnancies were normal, we would have babies at home. For our next baby, Jack, we planned a water birth. At the time, we did not understand that what you plan for a birth and what actually happens are not always synonymous. Jeannie labored in the tub, but Jack arrived in her arms on the way to the bedroom as the water was being refilled. I tried to explain to the newborn that he did it all wrong, but he really didn't seem to care and just fell asleep. Katie, Michael, and Patrick were much better listeners. They all arrived under water in the tub and were greeted by their brothers and sisters shortly thereafter. Jeannie recovered quickly after the births, so I didn't feel bad about asking her to "hurry up and clean the mess." Whenever people tell me "You go on stage and make people laugh—you must be brave," I always think of Jeannie. She really is amazing. So are midwives. If I ever give birth myself, I'm definitely going midwife.

I'm not antidoctor. I think there is way too much pressure on doctors these days to be God-like saviors, and as a result there is much arrogance in the medical community. Doctors always have the attitude of "Look, we are scientists—we've figured out the human body. Trust us." Yet whenever I go for a checkup, they are always like, "It's either a freckle, or we have to amputate your head. That will be five thousand dollars." I think most people's apprehension about home birth is the absence of the doctor. I mean, could you imagine if there was no doctor at Jesus's birth? That could have changed the course of history.

Newbornland

I'm not surprised by how much I love my children. I'm relieved. Shortly after I found out Jeannie was pregnant for the first time, I was worried. Would I be able to provide the unconditional love of a parent? I always found those Anne Geddes baby-flower photos annoying, and it kind of puts me in a good mood to see a teenager fall off a skateboard. How could someone like me ever hope to be a good parent? Even I knew my "Oh, what a cute baby" act was not very believable. What if I saw my baby and I was like, "Yuck!"?

If you are having these feelings, too, don't worry; it just means you're a horrible person. The good news is when your baby is born, something happens. I can't explain it. You just love your baby. Unconditionally. Even if you didn't get the baby thing before, when you experience your own, you immediately fall in love and feel like you could kill or die for that baby. I was born with a heart that was two sizes too small, but when I saw my baby, it was like the Grinch discovering the true meaning of Christmas.

The newborn stage is a special time. It's really a sacred time when nobody expects you to do anything except enjoy your new bundle of joy. This sacred time lasts roughly twenty minutes, and then you become the publicity agent for the mother and the baby. The masses of family and friends want to be assured the mother is okay and get information on the baby. For some reason, it's really important for people to know how much the baby weighs. This always baffled me. "How much does she weigh?" That's rude. She's not even a day old, and people seem to be obsessed with my daughter's weight? She was nine pounds, but I remember telling friends, "She was eight pounds, sixteen ounces" because it sounded thinner. Either way, she carried the weight very well, but we put her on that Atkins diet anyway. Of course, there is nothing anyone can do with the information about your newborn's weight. No matter what the weight, they say the same thing: "Oooh, big baby."

I don't have to explain that newborn babies are an enormous amount of work. When we had Marre, it was exhausting . . . watching Jeannie do it all. With each newborn, I was shocked at how much work there was. The infant just lies there sleeping, crying, or cooing, not even offering to help. I always think, "Great. We got another lazy one." Newborns are lazy. You even have to help a newborn burp. Of course then you have to try and stop them from burping for the next eighteen years.

But babies are worth it. It's amazing the power a baby

has over a parent. They are so cute even though they are ridiculously out of shape. I mean, I'm out of shape, but a baby? Please. They have zero muscle tone. They can barely hold their heads up. It's embarrassing, really. Still, they must have some kind of strange magic, because there is nothing that exists in the universe that can be as difficult, make you lose as much sleep, smell as bad, and still be so loved. Once on the road, I drove past a serious skunk smell, and my only thought was "I miss my baby."

Babies are adorable, but they kind of have to be because they are rude. "Waaaa." That's not polite. "Waaaa, waaaa, waaaa!" I don't speak baby, but my guess is there is no "please" in that statement. Babies are the worst roommates. They're unemployed. They don't pay rent. They keep insane hours. Their hygiene is horrible. If you had a roommate that did any of the things babies do, you'd ask them to move out. "Do you remember what happened last night? Today you're all smiles, but last night you were hitting the bottle really hard. Then you started screaming, and you threw up on me. Then you passed out and wet yourself. I went into the other room to get you some dry clothes, I came back, and you were all over my wife's breasts! Right in front of me, her husband! Dude, you gotta move out."

It's strange for a father when a mother breastfeeds. The baby always seems to look right at the dad like, "What are you going to do about it? Nothing. You're pathetic. Why don't you take a picture, weirdo?" When I complain about this to Jeannie, she thinks I'm being crazy, but I don't trust newborn babies. We really don't know them. We don't know what they've been doing in utero for nine months. They could be a terrorist, a communist, or, even worse, a book agent!

I think it's also weird how many babies go for the skinhead look. Don't take fashion advice from a baby. I tried to do the "onesie" thing last summer, and I'm not sure, but I think people were laughing at me. Anyone who has ever been the parent of a newborn baby knows that baby clothes are just plain stupid. I mean, they are cute for pictures, but after that, just take those stupid clothes off and wrap your baby in a towel. How much time and money would we save if we just wrapped them in towels? For those of you less concerned with the environment, paper towels would be even better.

Unfortunately you get tons of baby clothes as gifts. That is what people want to get you. Baby clothes are like torture for both the baby and the parent. Getting babies dressed up in those little clothes is a major struggle. The baby is screaming, and you are in a panic, so you are always putting their wrong leg in the armhole and the head through the leg hole. All the while, your baby is turning red and wailing, like, "Why are you doing this to me?" and you are just apologizing over and over again, like, "Shhh, I'm sorry, we're almost done, shhh, Grandma gave this to you and she wants to see you in it, shhh, oops, it's on backwards, I'm sorry, let me start over . . . shhh . . ." Then, when you finally get the clothes on, they usually throw up on them, or it is immediately time for a diaper change, and you have to start all over again.

Of course, what people should be giving newborns are diapers. Just diapers and coupons for free diapers. Newborns go through like a case of those a week. Giving a newborn clothes just makes no sense at all. Newborns can't dress themselves, and from what I've experienced, they never go out. Either that, or we've had some really homebody newborns. I've been around five newborns, and not one of them has said, "Tonight I'm meeting some friends for sushi—can you help pick out an outfit?" Fashion's Night Out is not a big thing for babies.

And the snaps and buttons never end. I always feel like I'm trying to put a duvet on a moving comforter. As I snap baby clothes, I can hear the employees at the baby clothing factory laughing at me: "Ha, ha, no, no, put twenty more snaps on, Bob. Ha, ha, ha! Now put on a snap that doesn't even have a matching snap. Ha, ha, ha, good one, Bob!" I'm sure there's someone named Bob working at the baby clothing factory. Well, at one time there probably was.

Instead of figuring out a way for baby clothes to have something less stupid than snaps, the geniuses named Bob at the baby clothing factories were busy designing something even more stupid: baby versions of adult shoes. My brother-in-law Patrick bought our then three-month-old Jack tiny Timberland hiking boots. Our baby couldn't walk, let alone hike. Patrick explained that the boots would be cute. Cute, yes, but only because they're ironic. A baby wearing construction-worker boots that weigh more than he does. Really, it's mean. It's like giving a blind person a microscope. "Look at him fumble with that. Isn't that adorable? I have to get a picture. He's holding it upside down."

Newborns always get gifts from your friends and family. New dads don't. I know, it sounded unfair to me, too. What did the newborn do? Nothing, right? The people giving the gift don't even know what the newborn would want. It's usually the first time the person is meeting the baby. How could they know the baby's taste? Usually they are not even gifts they can use.

Once someone got our newborn son a book. A book? Hello, the baby doesn't even speak English—how do you expect him to read it? Then I realized it was one of those cool touchy-feely books with barely any words. Like one page is felt, then there's like a crinkly page, then a silk one. Anyway, I stuck that book in my desk drawer for me to read later. That book was way too nice to waste on a baby. Please, just get them diapers.

Before I had kids, I was afraid of diapers. Now I am a diaper expert. At times I feel like a diapering professional. I can change a diaper standing, squirming, screaming, on an airplane, and even in the dark. And I can change a baby's diaper, too.

Changing a diaper in the middle of the night is a unique skill. It's like *The Hurt Locker*, but much more dangerous . . . and you don't have the two other guys on the elite squad to help you out. It's just you, the baby, and the wet diaper in complete darkness. Around 4 a.m., you'll hear the half-asleep cry from the baby. Allow me to take a moment to describe what a half-asleep baby is. Sleeping babies will often cry due to discomfort of some sort. If you can find a way to defuse the problem immediately, they will return to a fully sleeping state. If you miss this opportunity to intervene, even by seconds, the results can be devastating to an entire household.

Back to 4 a.m. The cry continues. Is it hunger or diaper? Always thinking contingency, I'll start warming a bottle in a coffee cup of microwaved water. You shall see how this will come in handy later. You must react quickly and with purpose to the baby's cries. If you don't, the consequences are simple. You'll be up for three hours with a tired, cranky baby. Like disarming a bomb, everything must be done in a stealth manner that will not fully wake the baby. You have to get in and out.

An experienced pro like myself will grab the aforementioned warmed bottle (see, I told you it would come back), a new diaper, some wipes from the wipe warmer, and one of those scented blue diaper bags that are not only impossible to open but make as much noise as microwaving popcorn. You have to use the scented bag, or in the morning your house will smell like a subway station on New Year's Day. With the *Mission: Impossible* theme song playing in my head, I position a bottle in the baby's mouth, carefully propping it with a pillow while I quickly undo forty-five snaps on the sleeper. I will have exactly twenty seconds to complete my task. I carefully peel back the adhesive tape on the sides of the old diaper. The cries grow louder as the bottle falls out of position. And louder still as the cold air hits the open diaper area. Will I make it? The once-warm wipes feel cold to the touch, but it's too late to back down. The ice-cold wipe further startles the screaming yet somehow still-sleeping baby. Then the diaper is on, tape fastened, and the bottle is repositioned. The hardest part is over. Disaster averted. But I'm not out of the woods yet. I commence resnapping the sleeper in complete darkness. I probably skipped a few, but who cares? The baby is silent. I raise the crib rail and tiptoe out of the room a victor, a hero. I stub my toe on the bouncy chair but muffle my yelp of pain. As I close the door, I hear only the drinking of the bottle and then suddenly, "Waaaah!" The diaper is wet again. *Mission: Impossible 2.*

Dogfight

Every year after Jeannie has her annual baby, I receive congratulations from friends and family. There's always one person who says, "Oh, you just had a baby. Yeah, we just got a puppy." What? In no other situation could you compare a human to an animal and people would actually be okay with it. You could never say, "Oh, you just got married? Yeah, I used to have a pig. Does your new wife like to roll around in mud, too? My pig loved that."

Of course, the dog-and-baby comparison is nothing new. Dog owners are sincere and mean no insult. Their dog is their "baby." But, of course, a dog is not a baby. It's a dog. I also understand some people prefer dogs to babies. We are raising our children in New York City, which is not the most popular place to have children. If you hear someone cooing, "Oh, how cute!" on the street in NYC, you better look down, because they are going to be referring to a dog.

It's a good thing babies have no idea how often they are compared to dogs. I would think that would be pretty insulting to the babies. Let me be clear. I love all animals. I love to pet them. I love to eat them. I'm an all-around animal lover, but besides the drooling and whimpering, your dog is not that similar to a baby. Take the smells, for instance. Babies are the two extremes on the spectrum of smell. They either smell like heaven filled with lollipops or like a microwaved cesspool. The cleanest of clean dogs still smells like a dog.

Allow me to list a few other differences:

1. Dogs come when you call their name.
2. The absence of birth control does not lead to pet ownership.
3. You don't have to worry about your dog ever becoming addicted to meth.
4. You do not have to save so your dog can go to college and then find out after they graduate that they want to be an actor.
5. If someone is pushing a baby in a stroller, they are probably a parent or a caregiver. If someone is pushing a dog in a stroller, they are probably insane.

In some ways, having a kid is easier than having a dog. When you go on vacation, you don't have to kennel your kids (although a kid kennel is an intriguing new business idea—you're welcome). You can stay in any hotel with your kids, and you don't have to hide them when room service comes. I mean, *sometimes* I do, but that's only because I'm hiding my fries from my kids. With children, you can look forward to a time when they eventually learn to feed and bathe themselves. If you give a dog a bar of soap and put it in the bathroom, it is going to eat the bar of soap. Dogs and kids are both affectionate, but dogs always have dog breath. Or soapy dog breath.

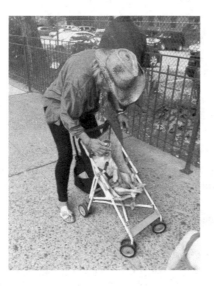

And I'm the weirdo with too many kids.

Occasionally, a dog will be presented as some training method for having a baby. "My girlfriend and I got a dog. We are going to see if we can handle that before we have kids." This is a little like testing the waters of being a vegetarian by having lettuce on your burger. Okay, maybe that metaphor doesn't make sense, but neither does using a dog as a training method for having a baby.

Circumcision

When you have a boy, you have to deal with the circumcision question. If you are eating a hot dog while reading this book, my apologies. Most men cringe when they hear the word *circumcision*. "Uh, can you talk about something else, like prison rape?" *Circumcision* is just a scary word. I looked up *circumcision* in the dictionary, and it just said: "Owwwww. From the Latin for Ow!"

Everyone will admit circumcision is crazy. The Germans flirted with the idea of making it illegal to circumcise your son. This is impressive, given Germans don't really have a great record on the human rights front. Obviously, circumcision began as a religious tradition. I don't know how they even came up with the idea of circumcision, really. I guess there was a meeting at some point.

LEADER: All right, how should we honor God?
GUY #1: I say we don't eat pork.

LEADER: I don't know. I like bacon. Anyone got anything
   else?
GUY #2: What if we cut off part of our penis?
LEADER: [*Beat.*] Okay, no pork. We'll go with no pork, and
   I want Guy#2 removed from this building.

Jeannie told me that in the Bible, Abraham circumcised
himself. Wow. I don't even like clipping my nails. Apparently
God told Abraham to do it. I would love to have overheard that
conversation.

GOD: Abraham!
ABRAHAM: Oh, hey, God.
GOD: I need you to do something for me.
ABRAHAM: Well, sure. You're God! Whatever you want.
GOD: I need you to circumcise yourself.
ABRAHAM: [*Beat.*] I think we have a bad connection here.
   You're breaking up. Can you send me an e-mail?

When you think about it, God's requests in the Old Testa-
ment took a dramatic leap in difficulty. "Don't eat that apple!"
"Build a boat!" Then, out of nowhere, "Cut off part of your
penis!" I imagine Abraham was like, "Uh, how about I build
two boats and no more bananas?"
   We have to assume Abraham went through with God's request. I'm not sure how Abraham hid this adjustment from his
wife. Maybe he didn't. Maybe he was getting out of the shower
and his wife was brushing her teeth.

WIFE: What the hell have you done?
ABRAHAM: Honey, I can explain . . . God told me to do it.

WIFE: What? What if God told you to jump off a bridge? What if God told you to sacrifice our firstborn son?

ABRAHAM: Actually, I have to talk to you about that one . . .

Circumcision is a tough decision for any parent. Do you put your newborn son through an enormous amount of unnecessary pain, or do you have a kid with an ugly penis? Unfortunately, Jeannie left the decision up to me. I decided to go through with it, but only because each of my sons requested it. Of course they didn't request it. I couldn't even discuss the decision with them, but I was pretty sure they didn't want someone clipping off part of their penis. I finally made the decision to do it for a number of reasons. One of which was fear. A friend recently had to circumcise their one-year-old because of repeated infections. Still enjoying that hot dog? Ultimately, I wanted my sons to be like their dad. Cut off from a little bit of their manhood.

The only thing worse than deciding to have your son circumcised has to be witnessing your son getting circumcised. I've had to watch my three sons go through this, and it haunts me to this day. I've blocked out most of it, but I'll never forget my first time. Well, my first son's first time. Well, hopefully Jack's only time. I remember everything vividly up until the point when I blocked everything out.

Since we elected to do a home birth, we didn't have the option of a quick circumcision after the birth, as in a hospital. We had to arrange a circumcision at home in our tiny apartment. Jeannie found a highly recommended mohel, Doctor Emily Blake, to do the procedure. Dr. Emily is a mohel, a doctor, and a rabbi. Talk about an overachiever. I was relieved to know my son's son-ness was in good hands. Then Jeannie notified me that she was going to invite some people to the ceremony. What? I didn't really want people to know we were even doing this to our precious newborn son, let alone throwing a party to announce it. I didn't even know we were Jewish. There were a dozen guests, including my sister's girlfriend, a priest, and our mohel/rabbi/doctor attending the ceremony. We literally had the beginning of a classic joke.

A priest, a rabbi, and a lesbian walk into a circumcision . . .

As I mentioned before, I completely blocked out most of what happened that night, as I did with the other nights my sons were circumcised. Of course, if they ever question why they were circumcised, I'll do the manly thing and blame it on their mother.

The Invasion

Nobody likes being a new kid. It's uncomfortable and strange. People are mean and call you "dog breath." Well, maybe that was just me when I was the new kid in fifth grade.

When a newborn baby arrives, he or she is the new kid. In a family with young children, it's not just uncomfortable and strange for the new kid, it's uncomfortable and strange for everyone. Sure, the new addition to the family is always celebrated and loved completely, but he or she brings change to the family unit. At the time of birth, suddenly there's another person in the room or, in the case of a home birth, in your bathtub. It's really a special time. While this event is magical and mystical for adults, for young children it can be overwhelming and confusing. A three-year-old can witness their mother's belly getting larger, and you can read them every book about a new sibling coming, but they are still surprised when the baby actually arrives.

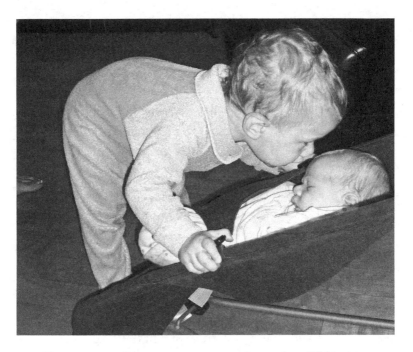

You are so cute I just want to . . . punch . . . okay, I'll kiss you.

For our one-year-old, Michael, the arrival of his younger brother, Patrick, was the shock of a lifetime and wildly confusing. As sweet and kind as Michael is, he still couldn't understand this small stranger who somehow just arrived and was stealing some of his thunder. He was gentle and kissed the baby's head the way we'd taught him to do with a doll before the birth, but when he looked to us for approval, there was some desperation in his big blue eyes. It was like the reaction of an aging chorus girl when the eighteen-year-old ingenue joins the show. "Welcome aboard. I hope you don't get injured."

Michael wasn't alone; all our children acted like they'd had a couple of Red Bulls after a breakup. Sleepless and clingy became their MO. Sibling jealously is always an issue, even if you have one kid dealing with the arrival of a new baby. I don't think any husband or wife would be thrilled if their spouse suddenly brought home another partner. "Bob, this is Frank. Frank will also be my husband." When you have four kids and a new kid shows up, the results are a little more dramatic. I guess only polygamist sister-wives could identify.

Jeannie and I attempt to make the transition as easy as possible on the kids. I try to be a compassionate dad. I always sit our other children down and explain that the new baby does not mean we love them any less, but we will have to let one of them go. I'm kidding, of course. There is nothing that can be said to a child to alleviate the stress of a new arrival. It can only be solved by one-on-one time and lots of cuddles. This is perfect, because you have all the free time in the world when dealing with a newborn. When newborns are not sleeping, they need constant attention. I think our youngest, Patrick, slept for a total of thirty-four seconds during his first three weeks.

What can we say to the other kids? "Okay, the bad news is we've hired someone to do your job, but the good news is you've been promoted to 'Former Cutest Kid.' Congratulations." The kids are not thrilled. With a new baby, it always feels like Jeannie and I are going through parental performance reviews. The other kids don't act out toward the baby, they act out toward us. It's not the baby's fault he's here. It's *our* fault. They don't know *how* we did it, but they know that *we* did it. Suddenly, our three-year-old starts sucking her thumb with a vengeance, looking at us like, "Mom didn't nurse me long enough. Now I will ruin my teeth so you will pay thousands of dollars in dental work." The first couple of weeks of a new arrival when you have four kids are like pledging a fraternity, except the parents are the ones being hazed. To make matters worse, there is no alcohol served during this process.

What about the new kid, Patrick? How did he adjust? He wasn't thrilled. Newborns don't smile, and they always give me that look of "Oh no, *you're* my dad?" Patrick went from having his own room in his "man cave" womb to being thrust into the center of a madhouse. He seemed to look around at our apartment, disgusted, as if to say "Wow. And I thought my *last* place was crowded." I know how you feel, my friend. I know how you feel.

Please take him. Take him now!

Eat the Coleslaw!

Even when I was a little kid, I always saw motherhood as an awe-inspiring occupation. My mom was always mothering my siblings and me. It was a twenty-four-hour-a-day position. Running errands, making dinner, picking us up, and yelling instructions from the other room. "Eat the coleslaw!" would be bellowed from the kitchen as we ate dinner. How did she know we weren't eating the coleslaw? Did moms have X-ray vision? We would giggle at crazy old Mom, but we knew that without her we were lost. All moms seemed simultaneously tireless and on the brink of exhaustion. Once when I was ten, I slept over at a friend's house. For fun, my friend and I decided that we would try to stay up all night. Around two in the morning, we thought we heard a monster. After drumming up the courage to investigate, we crept down to the basement to discover my friend's mom doing laundry in a neck brace. I remember thinking, "Maybe moms don't sleep. Maybe moms are indestructible!" Moms always seemed to be in a state of constant mothering. Conversely, I remember thinking all dads seemed like they were just returning from playing golf or about to leave to play golf. Maybe that was just the shirts men wore in those days.

Even back then, hats didn't fit my huge head.

Now, as a father, I have an even deeper appreciation for mothers. It's not just the endless tasks and limited sleep. Motherhood is filled with executive decisions, and with each decision comes possible conflict with kids, husbands, and other mom friends. With these other mom friends, there are so many opportunities for major disagreements and awkwardness. Let's say that a woman starts with twenty friends when she finds out she's pregnant. There is going to be awkwardness with, let's say, six of those friends because they have no interest in babies or are jealous she is pregnant. Then four won't agree with how she behaves during the pregnancy. She's too uptight, too casual, or not available enough as a friend. We are down to ten friends. Then there are the decisions of how the baby will be delivered, breastfeeding, circumcision, blanket or no blanket in the crib, and whether or when to return to work after the birth. These topics turn out to be more divisive than opinions about politics and religion. After a couple of kids, there might be one good friend left. And that friend is never available because she has too many kids herself. I'm amazed mothers have anyone to talk to. When a man finds out he's going to be a father, it barely covers more than twenty seconds of a conversation with his male friends. "I heard you two are expecting! Congratu . . . Who do you think is the best quarterback in the fourth quarter?"

Mothers need to talk, and fathers need to escape. I think this is why women of my mother's generation would go to ladies' luncheons. I remember as a teenager twice a year my mother announcing, "Me and the ladies are going out to lunch." She would return eight hours later . . . well, let's say, not sober. "Your father's a jerk! Now get me a gyro."

I suppose parenting wouldn't feel so overwhelming if Jeannie didn't make mothering look so easy. At times, I think she has more than two arms. She is an amazing partner and wife. The only thing Jeannie is missing is her own wife. A wife exactly like her. If you think this sounds sexist, you don't know Jeannie.

Since I am not "handy," Jeannie tends to do a lot of the inevitable household repairs that result from having five children who break everything. Recently, I was assembling a kid's scooter and futilely trying to shove the top piece in.

"Jeannie, do we have a hammer?"

"Yeah, we have like three hammers."

"Where are they?"

"In the toolbox."

"We have a toolbox?"

There is one exception to Jeannie's superhumanness. As capable, organized, and amazing as Jeannie is at almost everything, it is baffling how many times a day she loses her phone.

"Where's my phone?"

"Didn't you just find it?"

"Yes, but then I put it down somewhere. Can you call it?"

[*RING*]

"It's in your hand."

Jeannie calls this "mommy brain," but rather than condemning mothers as ditzy scatterbrains, I think it's just a matter of shifting priorities and focusing on the most important issues. Like taking care of me.

Jeannie is the mother of five children (six, if you include me) and my invaluable writing partner. I don't mean partner symbolically, like, "Oh, here's what the client's wife thinks." She is *the* partner. This is very rare in stand-up, so people are surprised that she is executive-producing my theater shows while being the mother of five kids. "Shouldn't your wife be home fat and miserable?"

We made that quilt together, too.

Jeannie comes from a family of nine kids, and she and her mother have really bonded over the trials and tribulations of being in this awe-inspiring position of mother. There is a certain language that only mothers can understand. They talk all the time on the phone, usually having the same five-minute conversation over and over again for like eight hours. When they aren't talking, I assume it's because Jeannie's lost her phone.

Toddlerhood

Toddlerhood is one of my favorite periods of childhood development, and not just because you can finally enter them in beauty pageants. (Don't worry, they do get used to the fake teeth.) *Toddler* is a term used to describe children ages one to three. Babies and toddlers are mostly what I've been exposed to at this point. I'm hoping parenting just gets much easier after this. It does, right? I know this is a book and I can't hear you, but I'm going to take your silence as a yes.

I used to wonder why I had hair on my legs, but now I know it's for my toddler sons and daughters to pull themselves up off the ground with as I scream in pain. Based on my experience, a baby will start walking at around eleven months . . . I think. Oh, jeez, I don't remember. I just know they start walking before they ride a bike and start smoking. All healthy babies eventually walk, but we treat those first steps like someone has just risen out of a wheelchair at a healing revival. "He's *walking*! It's a miracle!"

I guess walking is sort of impressive after ten months of just lying around. Actually, they don't immediately walk or even toddle. They "cruise" or hold themselves up with furniture in search of the hardest and sharpest surface to bang their head on. When they finally let go and take a few steps, it's more of a stumble or a stagger, like they are a drunken old man or a zombie extra from *The Walking Dead*.

What amazes me is that once they actually learn to walk, they are immediately trying to get away. You just say, "Time for a bath!" and they scoot away like they have an escape car outside. I don't know where they think they are going. They can't even reach the doorknob. I am always like, "What are you doing? You only know *us*! Think it through!" They've only been on the planet for twelve months, and they can't really go stay with a friend or check into a motel, but that doesn't stop them. It doesn't matter if they don't have a plan. They are just trying to leave.

Once your baby starts to walk you'll realize why cribs are designed like prisons from the early 1900s. This is clearly because toddlers are a danger to themselves. The main responsibility for a parent of a toddler is to stop them from accidentally hurting or killing themselves. They are superclumsy. If you don't believe me, watch a two-year-old girl attempt to walk up stairs in a long dress. It looks like a Carol Burnett sketch. Also, toddler judgment is horrible. They don't have any. Put a twelve-month-old on a bed, and they will immediately try and crawl off headfirst like a lemming on a mindless migration mission. But the toddler mission is never mindless. They have two goals: find poison and find something to destroy.

Toddlers love toilet paper. I mean, I love toilet paper, too—
who doesn't? Even the most devout conservationist can't live
without their toilet paper. "Reuse! Recycle! Wait . . . What?
We're out of toilet paper? Chop down that forest! Fast!" But
toddlers love toilet paper for all the wrong reasons. They have
no idea what it is for or how to use it, but they are passionate
about a nice, big, fresh roll of toilet paper. They love to play
with it, wear it, eat it, and, especially, unroll it. Leave a toddler
alone in a bathroom for five seconds, and they somehow unroll three hundred feet of toilet paper with supernatural speed.
Then you walk in and bust them, and they just look at you
like, "What? This stuff is obviously for me, right? It's right at
my eye level, and it's the most fun thing in the house." All the
geniuses at the Fisher-Price laboratories have yet to develop

I reckon a two-year-old is on the loose in these parts.

something as fun for a toddler as a ninety-nine-cent roll of toilet paper. Unfortunately for me, whenever this unrolling happens, it's always the last roll in the house. Have you ever tried to reroll an entire family-size roll of toilet paper? I just leave it in a big, undulating pile next to the toilet. I'm not going to throw it away. After all, it is still toilet paper.

After toddlers make the evolutionary leap to *Baby erectus*, you still end up pushing them in a stroller or carrying them most places if you'd like to reach your destination in the next decade. Fifteen-month-old Michael loves to run around, yet he always wants me to carry him everywhere in my sling. He is huge, but I can hardly feel my back breaking when I walk around with Michael in the sling because of the attention that he draws from everyone we encounter. I call Michael a "gateway" baby. Even people who don't like babies or children melt around his sweetness and charm. Michael makes the crabbiest New Yorkers smile. It's like I'm carrying the heaviest ventriloquist doll ever, but the routine is in gibberish.

The interesting thing that happens when walking around with a baby strapped in front of you at adult eye level is the baby acts like he thinks he is the one walking around and you are just this weirdo strapped to his back. He starts to have "conversations" with adults that you encounter. When babies move away from just the *mama-dada-baba* sounds, they start to make sounds that *could* be words, but they're not. It's the seriousness with which they deliver their baby talk that is the most entertaining. Michael's babble is delivered with the intensity and cadence of an Obama speech. People are compelled to respond in kind, but then Michael will just look at them like, "That's not what I said at all, you moron."

They make up for it when they turn two and they just start *talking*, and I mean talking all the time. It's as if all of those things they wanted to say before just come jumbling out in a whirlwind of botched sentences. They can't pronounce anything. "I wan pahk go down yittle swide eat appoo." I'm like, "C'mon, learn English. This is America, for God's sake!" When Katie was two, her English was so bad I thought she might be al-Qaeda. Some of this may have been because I when dressed her in a baby burka, she looked kind of suspicious.

Toddlers, for some reason, are always out of breath. They always sound like they have traveled by horseback for hours in order to deliver important news. "Mommy, Mommy, Daddy, [*breath, breath, breath*], I need to tell you something [*breath, breath, breath*] . . ." This news is so important, parental titles are unimportant. "Daddy, Mommy, Daddy! I need to tell you . . ." I'll chime in, "Yes, yes. What is it?" By that point, it will be apparent by the look on their face that they have completely forgotten what they even wanted to tell you. "Um . . . can I have some juice? I mean, I wet my pants." Toddlers also love to tell you secrets, especially when you are wearing a white shirt and they've been eating chocolate.

Everyone with a toddler has had that embarrassing moment when their kid will innocently yell a word in public that sounds like a really bad grown-up word. Once when two-year-old Jack was playing swords in the park with another boy, he yelled, "I'm gonna hit you with my big stick," but using the *d* sound instead of the *st*.

When Marre was two, I was in line at a crowded New York City grocery store, and I gave her a sippy cup of *juice* in a futile attempt to stop a meltdown. She bellowed at the top of her lungs, "I don't like jews!" Thank God, we live in New York City and my family looks like Hitler's fantasy. Otherwise, that would've been pretty awkward.

Jeannie has often described two-year-olds as at the peak of cuteness. For some reason, everything a toddler says is adorable. Maybe it's the squeaky voice. Maybe it's the made-up words: "Lasterday I had pesketti." or "It's waining! Can I bring my unclebrella?"

They can talk, but they can't exactly follow logic. Dr. Harvey Karp, author of *Happiest Toddler on the Block*, calls it the caveman phase. I've never known a caveman, but I guess that makes sense. You can't really reason with a two-year-old. There is a lot of redirecting: "Okay, instead of playing with the scissors, let's play with the ball. No, the hanging wineglasses are not a ball. Here, sit in this crib." Two-year-olds don't understand consequences. "If you keep taking off your shoes in the cab, you will lose your shoes!" Then you realize that's the point. They are trying to lose their shoes. That's why they are taking them off. The only consequences are for you. You will have to get them a new pair of shoes. Toddlers are adorable, but taking care of them doesn't really get easier. Whoever came up with the term "terrible twos" must have felt very foolish after their kid turned three.

Three-year-olds are just rude. They are still supercute, but now they are supercute *and they know it*. They have gotten supersmart, and they are not afraid to show it. It's like living with a child emperor. They act really entitled, bossy, and outspoken. They think the world revolves around them. I realize I'm describing myself, but somehow it works better for a three-year-old.

Recently I took my three-year-old, Katie, to the post office. As we were walking into the post office, a lady was walking out and stopped and smiled at little Katie. Katie took her thumb out of her mouth, looked the lady up and down, and said rudely, "What are *you* doing here?" This wouldn't have been so awkward, impolite, and funny if we knew the woman. We had never met or seen the woman before and didn't even know someone that looked remotely like the woman. In Katie's three-year-old world, this was an appropriate response to someone smiling at her.

Katie still sucks her thumb at three years old. When she was two, everyone told us that she would stop when she was three, but she kept on sucking her thumb. She is our third child and our first thumb sucker. Thumb sucking brings with it so many mixed emotions. There is that immediate fear that somehow we have failed her. That she is sucking her thumb because she doesn't get enough attention or she wasn't nursed long enough. The reality is that she probably gets more attention and has better parents than our first two kids. Still, why the thumb? Am I worried that one day the thumb will be replaced by a crack pipe? Yes. Is that likely to happen? No.

Thumb sucking is adorable in many ways. When Katie is angry, she uses the thumb sucking as an exclamation to emphasize her point. "I'm not taking a bath . . . [*insert thumb*]." When she has a stuffed-up nose, it is incredibly comical to witness her attempt to suck her thumb and breathe at the same time.

Of course, we've tried to stop her from sucking her thumb. We put some nasty goo on her thumb that she quickly got used to. She found a way to wipe it off and sucked the thumb with twice the vigor. We tried telling her to stop sucking her thumb because she was a big kid now, but that only made it more special and prompted Katie to do the double-handed thumb suck. She holds a protective hand over the hand that has the thumb being sucked. With the double-handed thumb suck, she still only sucks on one thumb, but it looks like she's playing a tiny harmonica. She then proceeds to hum quietly to herself as if to express her contentment with her thumb. We call this the thumb hum. At this point, I'm tempted to tell her to just start a toddler folk band.

Now that we have a new baby, we have been advised by our pediatrician that "she's only three" and to just let her suck her thumb so she can decide on her own when to quit. I wanted to put her on that thumb replacement patch but Jeannie said we should wait until she is four. Everyone knows that a thumb sucker at age four is destined for prison.

Toddlers are too cute to punish. They get let off so easy. They can behave abominably, but what's the worst thing that can happen to them? A time-out? Big deal. All I want to do is take a time-out. I was recently watching a football game with Katie, and the announcer said, "The Jets have asked for a time-out." Katie saw the quarterback talking to the coach and asked, "Why did he get a time-out?" I thought for a second and then just said, "Because he didn't listen to his daddy."

You don't have to worry about anything as a toddler. You don't get punished, everyone spoils you, and you have no job. You are treated like a king. I always say to my toddlers, "Enjoy it while it lasts! It's all downhill from here."

The more I'm around young children, the more I realize we are all just giant toddlers. I think we are always unconsciously seeking to return to our early childhood. This is why we go to bars. Now that I have little children, going to a bar is a completely different observational experience. Many bars have a dartboard, a pool table, and various board games. There is music, dancing, and singing along to karaoke. There are Jell-O shots, for God's sake. Think of the last two times you had Jell-O. When you were three and when you were in that bar in Florida for spring break. Have you ever turned off the lights in a room filled with children? They immediately start screaming and acting insane. Is it merely a coincidence that lights are so low in bars? It's just a license for adults to misbehave.

We go to bars so we can behave like children, toddlers, really. Have you been to a bar at two in the morning? You might as well be picking up a kid at nursery school. It's the same experience. The behavior's the same. In both places, there's always some strange yelling for no reason at all, "Whooo hooo! Wheeee!" or someone climbing up on a table and getting into trouble with the authorities. In both places, people break into song: "Sweet Ca-ro-line, Oh oh ohhh! Everybody! Oh oh ooo, Old MacDonald had a farm, E-I-E-I-OH!" You go into the bathroom at the bar and it's obvious some people aren't potty trained. In both places, there's usually someone crying, "She was my best friend! But not anymore! I want my mommy." Occasionally, a fight will break out: "He was standing where I wanted to stand. So I punched him in the head. I want more juice." Nursery schools and bars at 2 a.m. are the only places where it is completely normal if someone just spontaneously throws up on the floor . . . and just like a toddler, the bar patron wakes up the next day not remembering or caring how they behaved.

The Evil Within

Because I have children, I wash my hands. Of course, prior to children, I washed my hands, but now I *really* wash my hands. Surgeons would be impressed. I don't want you to think I'm a germophobe. I'm not at all. I'm just terrified of germs.

It begins when you become a parent. You wash your hands to protect your precious newborn from germs; then you wash your hands to protect yourself because little kids are walking petri dishes of different viruses. The only thing weaker than a toddler's handshake is their immune system.

Toddlers are a virus's best friend. Viruses are usually spread by close contact and saliva. If you look up the definition of *toddler*, the first thing it should say is "close contact and saliva." Toddlers are always the contagion. Our home becomes the CDC every winter. Jeannie is obsessed with having a clean house, but our kids bring home viruses like they are collecting them. The virus will go around the family, taking its sweet time. Taunting us: "Oh, you think I'm done? Hardly. Just got my second wind. I'm taking another lap."

You don't have to be a research scientist to figure out the origin of these virulent epidemics. They come from an experimental breeding ground specializing in the manufacture and mass dissemination of disease known as "the nursery school."

Picture an incubator filled with little germ-infested creatures crawling all over one another drooling and sneezing with their mouths open. Then draw them all into a tiny section of the incubator to use the "potty" and instruct them all to "wash their hands." Then have each one of them turn on the faucet with their well-traveled little fingers that each harbor a multitude of secrets; run them for half a second under icy water that serves as a refreshing drink to the busy bacteria who live and work on said fingers; then make sure the faucet is turned off with the same fingers that turned it on so any of the viruses and bacteria that may have taken a rest stop on that faucet handle can hop back on their tiny finger chariots to fulfill their manifest destiny. One last stop at the towel that everyone has wiped his or her hands and/or noses on, and a whole new generation of infectious disease has been born.

Did I mention "incurable"? There is nothing that you can do to prevent or cure these bugs that hit your family. Maybe with the first kid you will run to the doctor, but after that you know better. If you are dumb like me, you will be surprised to discover that antibiotics do not work on viruses. Turns out bacteria and viruses are totally different. They are not even distant cousins. No wonder I didn't get into medical school. I mean I didn't try to get into medical school, but if I did, I totally would have failed that question on the medical school test.

Your kid's doctor will always give you the same advice about the virus: "You have to let it take its course." In other words, "There's nothing we can do." So you return home to your flimsy bomb shelter totally vulnerable. Just waiting for the next inevitable attack.

I don't want to give the terrorists any ideas, but if I really wanted to cripple a city with biological warfare, my WMD of choice would have to be the toddler.

Secrets and Lies

I like to think of myself as a relatively honest person. It's usually just easier to be honest. However, the complexity of parenting leads you to lie to your children. Honestly, I'm shocked how often I lie to my children. Cute sentence, right? Maybe they aren't all lies. I suppose some of it is just dishonesty. Some of it's acting. Being a parent to a young child is being an actor. I've been lucky enough to act in movies, TV, and on Broadway, but I believe my finest acting moments have been with my children. Parents of young children are always acting. You act excited to read a story for the five-hundredth time. You act impressed someone went to the bathroom on the toilet. The excitement I show to some of the children's scribbles should get me a Golden Globe nomination. Of course, this parental acting is a necessary form of encouragement. Most parental lies just seems pointless and almost abusive.

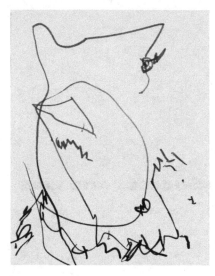

Great job, honey!

A man from the North Pole who slides down the chimney and brings presents seems so much more believable than a bunny that hides eggs. Somehow little kids believe all this stuff. It's pathetic, really, how gullible they are. I understand that we want them to experience some of the magic of childhood before they are forced to grow up and face the harsh reality of gas bills and root canals, but really? Some of these frauds that we purposely perpetuate are just unnecessary. A *fairy* that brings you *money* for your *teeth*? Who started that one? And why do we keep it going? We are totally pressured into telling this lie because we are terrified that if we are the only *honest* parents who say, "Look, you lost a tooth. Congratulations. Enjoy looking like a hillbilly. Here's a dollar," we might be unconsciously depriving our children of some yet unknown but really important stage of development, and we won't find out until it's too late and we find a dead hamster in their backpack.

By the way, could we all agree on the cash value of a tooth? I remember finding a shiny quarter under my pillow for my first tooth and being excited that I could buy a candy bar. I went to school for finance. I understand basic economics. When Marre lost her first tooth, I adjusted for inflation. According to my calculations, one dollar would be perfect. Marre was thrilled in the morning when she lifted her pillow to see George Washington frowning up at her. However, when she returned from school that afternoon, she was devastated. What had happened? Through her tears Marre choked out, "The Tooth Fairy hates my tooth! Why did Nellie get *twenty dollars* for her tooth!?" Because Nellie's parents didn't have change, that's why. Somehow we all get the memo that you can no longer put new babies to sleep on their stomach, but no one can agree on the value of a tooth? Come on, people.

Eventually, children start questioning these ridiculous lies. Marre, now eight, has begun to wonder how Santa can reach every house in the world by flying reindeer. I suppose soon Marre will start lying to Jeannie and me about believing in Santa a couple of years after she stops. That's what I did. I didn't want to ruin it for my parents, and also I didn't want to risk dissuading them from getting me presents.

I'm not proud of the lies I tell my children. Some are truly selfish and for the wrong reason. "Honey, you wouldn't want a bite of Daddy's cheeseburger. It's spicy." I don't feel guilty when I deny eating my kids' after-school snacks. I feel guilty telling them that their mom did. Of course, no parent sets out to lie to his or her children. I never did. Then again, I never thought I would let my three-year-old watch TV or chew tobacco. Sometimes we have to lie about stuff to scare them out of hurting themselves. "Don't play with firecrackers. My friend blew his hand off with a firecracker." In a few years they'll learn that *everyone's* father had a friend who blew his hand off with a firecracker. We will be revealed as the liars we are, and to retaliate against our hypocrisy, our children will grow up and lie to their children.

Every parent lies to their kid and that is a fact. We don't want to, but we do. The biggest lie we usually tell is when we threaten our children not to lie. "Don't lie or I'll tell Santa."

"Why isn't this the same guy from the mall?" —*Marre, age six*

A Critical Analysis
of Children's Literature

Everyone knows you are supposed to read to young children. Well, that's what I hear when I have my kids watch *Sesame Street* so I can waste time on the Internet. "Read to your children." Interestingly enough, when you hear "Read to your children" on *Sesame Street*, they never say, "Did you hear me? Do not watch *Sesame Street*! Turn off the TV and read that kid a book!" We know we are supposed to read to our kids—what they don't tell us is that we will be reading the same books over and over and over again. Around the tenth time reading some of these books to your kids, you begin to develop some really strong opinions and questions about them.

- *The Very Hungry Caterpillar:* I'm sure I'm not the only one who is concerned that maybe the main character has an eating disorder. Hey, I identify.

- *Five Little Monkeys:* I'd think that after the second little monkey jumped off the bed and bumped its head, the doctor who the mama called would have been tempted to call Children's Services. Yet the doctor's advice remained, "No more monkeys jumping on the bed." Really? Didn't that doctor take an oath at some point? I smell a lucrative malpractice suit.

- *The Giving Tree:* A favorite, but, really, how depressing. Whenever I read this to my children, I always think, "I'm the tree. I'm the tree. Now I'm the stump." What's the lesson here? Take everything from your parents until they have nothing left, and then move back in when you've squandered it all and you're an old loser, and your parents will let you crash on their stump.

- *Caps for Sale*: Another favorite, but why would anyone want to buy a cap that someone is already wearing on his head? If there are monkeys in a tree, where is this peddler selling these hats? Where are the people? I've read this book a hundred times. He's not going to sell any of those caps. He should just let the monkeys keep them. They are the only ones that want them anyway.

- *Goldilocks and the Three Bears:* No one ever questions why the Papa Bear and Mama Bear slept in separate beds. What was going on in that marriage? More backstory needed.

- *The Wheels on the Bus:* I'm not sure if *Wheels on the Bus* started as a book, as a song, or as a torture technique, but it sounds like it was a pretty annoying bus ride.

- *Goodnight Moon:* He has to say "goodnight" to everything in the room? That kid was obviously just procrastinating. How manipulative.

- *Harold and the Purple Crayon:* Great book, but where do I send Crockett Johnson the bill for cleaning my walls? Glad it wasn't *Harold and the Purple Book of Matches.*
- *The Runaway Bunny:* Who wouldn't want to run away from that mother? Talk about overbearing.
- *Go, Dog. Go!:* It gets heavy with the "Do you like my hat?" subplot but is a really, really easy read. Totally my pace. The message is clear, concise, and important. Everyone wants to go to a party in a tree. It's true!

My children teaching me to read.

- All Dr. Seuss books: Is it possible to read a Dr. Seuss book and not sound a little drunk?

This brings up another aspect of reading to your children. You are not just reading. You are performing, or at least you're supposed to be. Jeannie has well-defined characters, each with a complex history. I suffer by comparison. I've had one of my kids tell me to read with "less boring."

Every parent has his or her favorite children's book. They often sound passionate about the book. "I just love *Babar*." It's not that *Babar* is so good, it's just that most children's books are so bad. Many children's books don't even feel like first drafts. They feel like someone has sent the text of most children's books via Morse code. "Tom has a ball. Cindy has a doll. Tom and Cindy are friends. End of book. Stop."

Don't get me wrong, I have great memories of children's books, and my reading level has not advanced far beyond them. It's just when I pick up one of my old favorites, I'm sorry, but it never holds up. For example, my favorite book as a child was *Harry the Dirty Dog*. The story goes like this: Harry was a white dog with dark spots who didn't like to take baths. He ran away and got very dirty, becoming a black dog with white spots. Eventually he gets hungry and tired and wants to go home. Upon his return, his family doesn't recognize him because of the color change until he gets a bath and they realize it is Harry. Really? They don't recognize a dog that outside of color looks identical to their dog, does the same tricks, and is obviously dirty? I'm sorry, I just don't buy it. How dumb do they think I am? And I'm pretty dumb.

To be fair, some of them hold up. *The Little Engine That Could.* I still never think he's going to make it up the mountain, but I'm always pleasantly surprised when he does. It's kind of the *Rocky* of children's books. Still waiting for the sequel, *The Little Engine That Sought Revenge: Part Deux.*

No Further Questions

I often wonder what my young children really think of me. I can be silly and playful, but at times I do have to be "a bad, mean daddy." For example, I rarely give them one more chance. If they are not getting dessert, they are *not* getting dessert. I have actually turned the car around. I try not to be mean, just strict. And they let me know. From the moment my children learned to speak, I've heard many different versions of "You are a bad, mean daddy" in reaction to my strict style. Just when I start to worry about being remembered as a tyrannical figure, my children remind me in their unique style of communication that I am not, in their eyes, the dictator that I think I am.

Negotiation seems to be the predominant form of communication in my daily dealings with my children. "Dad, if I take a bath, can I watch a movie?" "What do I get if I clear the table?" I always seem to be on the losing end of arbitration. I constantly feel like I'm bartering with my children. I suppose this is part of the parent-child dynamic. I'm sure that throughout the centuries, sons and daughters have bartered with their fathers and mothers. I wonder if Jesus negotiated with God about some of the stuff he had to go through.

"Jesus, you are dying on the cross for all Mankind."

"Well, if I do that, can everyone have Sundays off?"

Notice the response is always a question. The question is the primary form of communication for little kids. They learn to speak, and the questions commence. Anyone with kids knows about the questions. "Daddy, what are you doing? Daddy, why are you doing that? Daddy, how long are you going to be doing that? Daddy, why are you putting on headphones and having a beer for breakfast?" I sometimes believe preschool was created by a parent who needed a reprieve from the incessant questions of a three-year-old.

Of course, these never-ending questions require answers you are not qualified to give. How do you answer, "Daddy, why are you a stand-up chameleon?" or "Why don't dogs get the chicken pops?" When my son Jack was four, he pointed to a car antenna and said, "Look, Daddy, stick." I clarified: "Actually, that is an antenna." Jack then asked, "What's an antenna?" After realizing I had no idea how an antenna worked, I explained, "It's a . . . stick. A metal stick. You nailed it, buddy."

Even all their so-called statements will contain a question in the subtext. "I'm hungry" is really "Why don't you feed me?" "I have to go to the bathroom" is "Can you clean up this pee on the floor?"

Another endless form of questioning is under the "Are we there yet?" category. If you ever mention something fun that you are going to do with your young children, and there is any time that will elapse between the *very moment* you bring it up and when you are actually doing the fun thing, you will be barraged with questions during that entire time period. If you tell them that you might go to Disney at some point in the coming year, you have opened a Pandora's box.

"Are we going to Disney now?" "How long 'til we go to Disney?" "Is it time to go to Disney yet?" "How many more hours 'til we go to Disney?" "What does 'three months' mean?" "Is it three months yet?" It is crucial that you withhold as much information as you can about this fun future event until thirty seconds before you arrive. Or ten seconds, depending on your question tolerance.

Out of necessity, all parents of little kids actively attempt to curb the unnecessary questions by speaking in parental code to each other. Parents will write notes, whisper, or spell things in front of their children. Once Jeannie said, "Don't tell anyone about the i-c-e c-r-e-a-m." I remember thinking, "Who's in the emergency room? And why do I want a Dilly Bar?"

Of course, there are many things you shouldn't say or do in front of a three-year-old. Everyone knows you're not supposed to argue or curse in front of young children. What you'll learn is the only time a parent really needs to argue or curse is when they are with young children. If you don't believe me, wait until your kid spills a drink on your computer. We tried a "cursing mug" where if Jeannie or I cursed, we'd have to put money in the mug. Two hours later, our son threw a ball and accidentally broke the mug. And, yes, I cursed when he broke it. Even more important than not arguing or cursing, a parent should never say the words "ice cream" in front of young children. Little kids only hear a commitment. "Yeah, I'll have ice cream." You can't explain to them, "Daddy was just saying the words 'ice cream.' It doesn't mean we are having it right now. Do you understand?" They will, of course, nod and say, "I'll have chocolate." I'm not exaggerating about saying "ice cream" in front of a three-year-old. Test my theory at your own peril. You don't believe me? Go on, try it. I dare you. Have you done it yet? See, I told you. Now don't you wish you had followed my advice? Wait, you didn't really do it, did you? I feel like I can't trust you anymore.

Bring in da Noise

The definition of children should be "young humans constantly making noise." Whoever first coined the phrase "the pitter-patter of tiny feet" to describe the noise that young children make was way off. That is like confusing a stick with a forest.

If children equal noise, then having five kids is like living on a construction site. Noise from our children is a constant in our house. Silence is startling to me at this point. Once, a moment of silence actually woke me up: "What's that? Is a tsunami about to hit?"

Like an orchestra that is always rehearsing, my children provide a wide variety of sounds. There should be a children's song "If you're happy and you know it, keep it to yourself and let your dad watch the football game." There's crying, humming, tapping—and that's just when they are asleep. My son Jack actually makes noises of video games in his sleep: "*Beep, peep. Ba too! Ba too!*" The scary thing is we don't have a Play-

Station, an Xbox, or a Wii, although he asks for one daily. He is actually dreaming about playing video games. Well, we all can dream.

The good news is that the night noises are barely audible from another room. They just mix in with the other city sounds. The bad news is that the night is quickly over. The worse news is that children are at their loudest in the morning. Of course, it's not just the mornings, it's all the time. I'm pretty confident I'll never have to tell my children to speak up. Our apartment may be small, but at least our children talk like they are on a helicopter. Maybe this is why grandparents eventually lose their hearing. It's not age. It's necessity. Why do you think grandparents love your children so much? It's because they're half deaf.

I don't want to give the impression there is any consistency to the noise levels—we are talking about children, after all. There are different volumes of loud, and kids know their cues. If you get a phone call, children intuitively know to speak louder, based on the importance of the call. If you are removing a toddler from a wedding or a funeral, they will understand they are supposed to scream. This is why there's virtually no difference between carrying a two-year-old and playing the bagpipes. You might as well be wearing a kilt.

Screaming. Did I mention the screaming? Screaming is usually associated with horror films and roller coasters. This is why I usually look like I've just watched a horror film on a rollercoaster. Kids love to scream. Frightened, happy, bored. They scream. I've actually learned to love the sound of a vacuum cleaner. It's just so peaceful.

It's amazing how you get numb to a certain amount of the screaming. I've learned to focus on work with screaming in the background, like a surgeon in a MASH unit while being shelled. Incoming!

You also learn to decipher the many types of screaming. I've had thoughts like "That's the 'I had too much sugar' type of screaming." "Oh, that's an 'I don't want to take a bath' type of screaming." Then there's the "Did someone just get their hand caught in the door . . . let me get out of bed and run and find out" type of screaming.

There is a tipping point with screaming where the screaming eventually becomes contagious. If one kid starts screaming, even the children that were docile or napping start screaming. I was never a screamer, but now I scream. Well, maybe I'm not screaming, but I raise my voice over really important things like washing hands. Initially, I was shocked. Wait, why am I raising my voice? Now I know. I yell because my kids don't hear me otherwise. To them, my normal voice doesn't register. They only hear, "Carry on. Don't acknowledge I'm even talking to you. Carry on." Unless, of course, I scream.

If you come to visit us at our apartment building, there is no need to ask what apartment we live in. Just follow the screaming.

An amazing source of income.

The Chud People

Like many of us, I grew up in the type of neighborhood where you had to go outside and look in your neighbor's driveway to see if anyone was home. In New York City, if you live in an apartment building, there are likely people living beside you, below you, and above you. You can hear your neighbors leave for work and come home at night. You know their traffic patterns and when they take a shower. Sometimes you can hear when they are arguing or even when they have a cough. The unspoken NYC apartment etiquette is that neighbors should make every effort not to deliberately disturb each other or look each other in the eye.

Many people in New York live above or next to a bar or a nightclub, and I am sure that is incredibly annoying. I am also sure that the nightclub scenario would become much more attractive if one were faced with a choice between that or living in the apartment under my family.

We have five small children climbing, jumping off furniture, throwing themselves on the floor in a fit, and for no reason at all just tapping. Not to music. Just tapping. No reason. Just tapping. Tap, tap, tapping. Annoying, right? We've lived in our apartment for six years, and we are on our third set of downstairs neighbors. Living there presently are two brothers from Italy who seem to be visiting the U.S. less and less since moving into the apartment. Hopefully we are not damaging our country's relationship with Italy.

We make efforts to stop our children from making noise, but it's like trying to stop the sun from coming up. We've explained to them that there are people living downstairs. We explained that our neighbors don't like the knocking and the bouncing of a basketball at 7 a.m. on Sunday morning. We have explained and explained and explained, but alas the thumping continues. In the entire time we have lived in the apartment with our children, there was only one incident when I could even temporarily stop the incessant banging. I was telling my then four-year-old daughter Marre that she couldn't jump up and down because she was disturbing the people living below us. Suddenly she stopped and looked at me very seriously and said, "Wait, there are people living *in* the floor?" Thinking fast, I replied, "Of course there are people living in the floor. They are called the Chud people, and they get angry when they hear noises. Please don't wake them up or else they will climb up here and come after us!" Evil? Yes. But it freaked her out and stopped the noise for at least an hour, at which point she forgot about the Chuds and resumed jumping up and down. Progress, not perfection.

When the neighbors living below us inevitably decide to move out, they always make the polite request that we hide our existence from potential new tenants. We comply because we feel horrible for having had them suffer under the weight of our world for a couple of years. We agree to help them trick new neighbors into moving in below us just like we agreed to help our former downstairs neighbors trick *them* into moving in below us. We are very ethical in our dishonesty.

Hiding the fact that our apartment is essentially a nonmovable clown car is not easy. We must remove all proof of children from the hallways. This involves taking in scooters and strollers into our already cramped apartment. We scour the halls for any telltale plastic toy or a dropped goldfish cracker. We remove our children's holiday artwork from the front of our door. Our pre-Italian downstairs neighbors, Steve and Andrea, actually offered to buy us lunch so my family wouldn't even be in the building during an open house. A really kind way to say, "Just get the hell out of the building!" I thanked them for the kind offer and instead took it upon myself to get our chaos the hell out of the building for a couple of hours.

There was once a surprise visit by a very serious prospective tenant. Our neighbors called us at the last minute. We really had to scramble. It was too late to take the kids out for fear of exiting the building and running into the unsuspecting buyer with a gaggle of foot-heavy toddlers. When we heard the Realtor in the hallway with the nice couple, we shooed all the kids into a back room and told them they had to play "the quiet game." I forgot at the time that a two-year-old does not understand the rules of "the quiet game" or any rules of any game.

I clapped a hand over her mouth, and suddenly it became the scene in *The Sound of Music* where the von Trapp family is hiding in the convent from the German SS.

As we continue our search for a new apartment, our "must have" list does not include anything about "prewar," "original moldings," or "good neighborhood schools." We just need to find a place where the downstairs neighbors are deaf or some other example of people who can't hear that is not offensive to deaf people. Either way, I just don't want those Chuds to come after us.

Monsters

Kids are actually afraid of monsters. I remember being afraid of monsters as a kid, but now it seems pretty absurd. My son Jack is a confident, outgoing six-year-old, yet at night, monsters are a sincere concern of his. He's not making it up to get attention. To him it's a realistic possibility that there is a monster in the hallway, and he needs me as a security escort to go to the bathroom. He is not at all concerned about a domestic terrorist attack or an economic disaster, but he is terrified of monsters.

Personally, I think that the concept of an old white guy with a beard in a red coat coming down a chimney in the middle of the night or a fairy with a tooth fetish sliding things under my pillow while I sleep would be way freakier, but no, for kids it's monsters.

Monsters are no different from fear of the dark. Why are children afraid of the dark? Because monsters live in the dark.

You can tell a kid there is no such thing as monsters, and they will look at you like you are naive. "Right, Dad. There are no monsters. And we didn't really go to the moon either." And they walk away from you like, "Don't say I didn't warn you." Where does this fear come from? It's just the fear of the unknown. They can't describe the monsters nor can they verbalize what these monsters will do to them if they ever actually do encounter them, but they know they're out there. Watching. Waiting. We never really completely lose the fear, but as adults we just give the monsters different names, like "Bankruptcy" and "Cancer." If our stockbrokers and doctors lived in our house, we'd be running to their room every night, too.

Of course, some kids aren't afraid of monsters at all. My three-year-old, Katie, wants to sleep in her bed with monster dolls and be told stories of zombies and werewolves. Maybe she is just the type of person who literally is "embracing her fears." I'm not exactly sure why one kid in particular is so scared of monsters, but he's waking me up almost every night to tell me they're there. And like any good parent, I explain to him that there are no monsters, but if he doesn't get back in bed, I'm going to let the monsters in his room.

Nothing in Common

I'm not a man with many hobbies. Besides eating, sleeping, watching an occasional football game, and, of course, eating, I just like spending time with my children, although I'm consistently amazed at how little I truly have in common with them. I'm comfortable with the fact that a two-year-old doesn't really grasp the "hide" or the "seek" part of hide and seek. And I'm not expecting to watch *The Wire* with an eight-year-old, but I would think there would be some overlap in interests. I realize their time on this planet has been short and sophistication is not something they can even pronounce, but I'm constantly stunned by our lack of commonalities. Nothing in my life has ever been as important as pushing the elevator button is to my three-year-old.

My six-year-old son, Jack, actually doesn't like mashed potatoes. Yes, mashed potatoes, one of the greatest things on earth. The ice cream of potatoes. I know, I didn't think it was

possible either. He of course loves french fries, hash browns, and baked potatoes, but mashed potatoes might as well be sewer sludge. "Ewww, mashed potatoes!" Little kids simply have bad taste in everything.

Little kids' taste in clothing is baffling. I'm not a big believer in fashion, but I know that if you ask a three-year-old boy to pick something out to wear to the park, the outfit will definitely clash and most likely not include pants. "Okay, why don't we wear pants and a shirt instead of a pair of goggles and a hat."

Little kids are the only sober human beings for the past fifty years to enjoy a parade. And it's not for kitsch appeal. People walking down the middle of the street to a drumbeat are fascinating to them. I always end up with the heaviest kid on my shoulders, watching the back of someone's neck get sunburned. It's no picnic.

Any time you eat outside with a kid, it's a "picnic." Kids love picnics, or, as I call them, "eating uncomfortably on the ground while swatting flies away from your food."

Little kids' taste in music is just as baffling. That Barney song, really? It's a total rip-off of a million other bad songs, and *Barney* gets the credit? I smell a lawsuit. My three-year-old daughter, Katie, figured this out subconsciously because she frequently does her own mashups of these obviously plagiarized tunes.

[*Singing*] "I love you, you love me, we're a happy fam-i-ly, with a knick-knack paddy-whack, give a dog a bone, this old man . . . is com-ing to town!"

They love all these horrible songs that are often about

other people's misery. Everyone knows that "Ring Around the Rosie" is about people dying of plague. The "Old MacDonald" song is clearly about some poor farmer who lost his farm to foreclosure. He *had* a farm. Why doesn't he have a farm anymore? The economy. Yet little kids smile and clap as they sing it. It's just cruel.

A small child's taste in movies is just as atrocious. You know you'll do anything for your kids when you find yourself paying twelve dollars a ticket to see *The Smurfs*. If you liked some of the movies toddlers liked, you'd definitely keep it to yourself. I brought my kids to see *Yogi Bear*. At the end, my then four-year-old son, Jack, popped out of his chair and said, "That was amazing!" I responded with the appropriate "Shhhh. Save the enthusiasm for a Pixar movie. This room is filled with your peer group. Don't embarrass yourself." I was tempted to turn to the parents behind me and announce, "He's being sarcastic."

Of course, I shouldn't be surprised when my children beg to watch *Spy Kids 2* for the twentieth time. After all, they are still impressed by a carousel. Also known as a "Merry-Go-Round" or "A Boring Piece of Junk." Forty years after man walked on the moon, a slowly rotating plastic statue garden will put my children in gleeful hysterics. "Yea! A merry-go-round! Daddy, can we go on it? Oh please, please?" You are just going around and around at an excruciatingly slow pace to music they wouldn't even play in an elevator. Nothing exciting is going to happen. That's why those bogus shabby leather seat belts are so loose. They will never have cause to need those seat belts. At least with NASCAR, there is always the potential for an awesome wipeout.

Katie enjoying the rotating pieces of junk.

I guess I'm doomed to never have anything in common with my kids except my last name. The sad thing is that by the time they're old enough to have good taste, I'll be one of those old guys with bad taste. "Really, Dad? *Those* clothes? *That* music? The Smurfs movie?" I finally understand what the Generation Gap is. Well, at least we'll always have McDonald's.

Hotel New York City

We live in a five-story walk-up. To you non–city dwellers, the term *walk-up* is used to describe an apartment building that is so luxurious, it doesn't have an elevator. It's called a "walk-up" because once you get up to your place, you never want to walk down. To fully understand this quandary, imagine you are watching television without a remote control and to change the channel you have to walk up five flights of stairs carrying a stroller. My dreams often involve elevators.

I should mention this apartment is on the Bowery in Manhattan. For those readers not presently recovering from heroin addiction who are familiar with this area of New York City, consider this: supposedly the term *hobo* comes from a description of the sketchy characters who were the main inhabitants on the cross streets of HOuston and BOwery. Hey, that's right where I live. Isn't that cool, hip, and ironic? The tiny overcrowded apartment where I'm raising my young children is in the same location where they manufacture homeless people. Location, location, location.

I truly love living in New York City, and I'm proud to call it home. New York is a global city and exerts a significant impact upon commerce, finance, media, art, fashion, research, technology, education, and entertainment. New York is the home of the United Nations and has welcomed all kinds of different cultures. Most recently, the parent culture. Despite the great improvements in the quality of life over the past couple of decades, the city is still not really kid-compatible.

The last several years have seen more and more parents deciding to stay in the city rather than take a long, frustrating, traffic-congested commute in for work. There have been a lot of great new playgrounds, kids' programs, and kid-themed events added to this fine city. These things coupled with all the other assets I mentioned earlier would make it sound like an ideal place to raise a well-rounded individual. The problem is that all these amazing places and activities that New York City has to offer are impossible to get to if you have five kids.

We don't have a car, an SUV, an eight-passenger van, or one of those *Partridge Family* buses. This means our primary forms of transportation are cabs, walking, and the subway. Cabs are probably the most convenient way to get around New York. True, cabs are superexpensive, but not really, compared with gas and parking. Cabs give you door-to-door service, and the drivers are always great characters. Why not just take cabs everywhere? Well, New York City cabs are only allowed to carry up to four passengers at a time. That's right, I can't fit my entire family in one cab. There goes the cab option. So, walking.

Walking had always been one of my favorite things about New York City. Many times on a balmy autumn evening I would opt for walking home from a spot at a local comedy club even if I could get home much faster on the subway. True, I am a cheap bastard, but it wasn't just because of the $2.25 that I could save. Walking for thirty minutes in the city is a completely different experience from walking for thirty minutes past a boring cornfield. There are remarkable sights, sounds, and people watching that make the time pass extraordinarily fast, and before you know it, you have arrived at your destination. However, when you add a couple of kids and a stroller to that equation, it becomes a vastly different experience.

Strolling a kid down a sidewalk seems like it would be easy except for the fact that the stroller is the Bermuda Triangle of kids' shoes. Strollers should always come with a coupon for a free pair of shoes. You can't stroll a kid half a block before they only have one shoe on. You have no idea when or how they got it off or how you missed a shoe being dropped or flung from something you are pushing right in front of you. Wouldn't you have walked over it? Toddler shoes should definitely come in threes. Of course, then you would always lose the wrong one. Then there are the kids that are "walking" with you. Little kids have short legs and complain a lot. Also when you walk with kids, they get bored of simply "walking" real quickly. Every metal grate, fire hydrant, tree guard, pole, and stoop becomes part of his or her personal obstacle course. A simple walk becomes *my* personal obstacle course . . . but my obstacle is actually *getting* anywhere while I try to wrangle my chimps off of dangerous death traps like tree guards, stoops, ramps, and poles and try to prevent them from getting too close to the curb, where giant trucks and mindless cyclist are inches away from plowing them over. So, the subway.

The subway is a fast and economical way to get around Manhattan, but from the moment the turnstile smacks your kid in the head to the time your child terrifies you by almost falling in the gap between the platform and the train, to the lack of interest anyone has in yielding a seat to you, to the kid inevitably *licking* the subway pole that 800 million filthy hands have touched, to almost missing your stop because it's too crowded to get off and you don't want your kid trampled, to carrying the stroller up three flights of subway station stairs behind people who are moving so slow you have to hold yourself back from stabbing them, to the time you realize that the museum is closed for renovations, this fast, economical, environmentally friendly form of transportation becomes more of a treacherous pilgrimage than a way of getting from point A to point B.

Why people are frightened to ride the subway.

So the payoff of all these terrific playgrounds, music classes, and cultural destinations dramatically diminishes when by the time you get to them you are a harried shadow of your former self. And instead of being enthusiastic about showing your children all the ancient artifacts in the Temple of Dendur, all you can do is feel terrorized anticipating the dread of the return trip, and you'd pay a billon dollars for some ruby slippers you could click together and magically be face-first in your bed in an air-conditioned room crying your eyes out, muttering over and over again, "There's no place like home!"

Raising children in New York City is just stupid. So why do we stay in New York City? Why don't we move to the suburbs or LA? Or at least get a bigger apartment. Well, I feel like I can't leave New York City. Los Angeles? I don't want to deal with the sunscreen, plus I can't get in that kind of shape. Besides I love New York City. When I was ten years old in Indiana, I remember looking around thinking, "There's been an enormous mistake. I'm not supposed to be here." I belong in New York City. I need New York City's energy, diversity, and the convenience. Sometimes I leave for work ten minutes before I have to be onstage. I don't want to give that up. I work in NYC during the day and at night. I'd be commuting constantly. Also there is no "normal" in New York City. I grew up in a small town where everyone was white and Christian and Giovanni's Italian restaurant was considered ethnic food. I want my children to be exposed to social, economic, and cultural diversity. I like it when my five-year-old asks me if a woman in a burka on the subway is a ninja. Jeannie and I would love to be in a bigger apartment, but we need something that would give us that last influx of cash to afford a place we really require. Something like selling a book that lots and lots of people might buy. Thank you for helping us getting a bigger home. Tell your friends. I'd invite you over to the new place, but that would mean I'd have to put on pants.

Vamanos

Recently on a warm, sunny day, a day perfect for napping rather than wasting outside, I found myself preparing to singlehandedly take all five of my kids to the park. I was doing this because I'm a great father and because Jeannie told me to do it.

Now, the only thing harder than leaving Jeannie and the kids when I go out of town to do shows is getting my entire family to leave the house to do anything. It is probably easier to land a quadruple jump in ice-skating than to get my five children to depart our home in a timely manner.

Everyone knows leaving anywhere with a large group is extremely difficult. I don't know how Moses did it. "Does everyone have their shoes on? I wanted to leave Egypt for the Promised Land like two days ago!" I grew up in a big family, so I learned early on that everyone leaving the house together at the same time is virtually impossible, and I'm sure there is some law of science to explain it: whereby if one body exerts force on five other bodies, no body goes anywhere. When I was growing up, my dad would just leave without us. I remember my mother saying, "Where is he? He left?" I remember thinking at the time, "Jerk." Now I get it.

When you have little kids, you can't just say, "C'mon, let's go!" and walk out the door. Nor can you say, "We're leaving in five minutes!" and sit down and check e-mail. It will immediately become apparent that even if you're taking them somewhere they want to go, your children will not move a muscle to do anything to get themselves ready. You must be an active participant in herding them out the door. If there is an electronic media device turned on anywhere in the vicinity, you must turn it off in order for your children's brains to process that you are speaking to them. Even if there were shoes lined up next to the door, at least one shoe from each pair will have mysteriously disappeared by the time they have to go on their feet. You must always add "find the shoe" time to your calculation of estimated time of departure. If you have a child in diapers, you must realize that they time their soiling of the diaper to the precise moment you say, "Okay, we are all finally ready to go!" If it's winter and there are hats, gloves, scarves, and mittens involved, just forget it. You might as well just stay in. It will be the spring thaw by the time you get them bundled.

It's not just leaving; it's leaving with stuff. There is just so much stuff to bring when you have young children. When you're headed to the park, you must pack diapers, wipes, juice boxes, and sunscreen. And then there is the stuff for the kids. (Thank you, I'm here all book.)

Once you have collected all the stuff *you* need for the kids, you must deal with the stuff that the kids have decided that *they* want to bring with them. It's never the logical thing to bring to the park like a bat or a ball. "Daddy, I want to bring my Play-Doh to the park." Your departure becomes further delayed by the twenty-minute debate you are forced into, where you futilely try to explain why Play-Doh, board games, and dress-up clothes are probably not appropriate things to bring outdoors. I usually compromise by allowing them to grab one toy they don't mind not returning with if it's lost or because it's Play-Doh.

My one-toy policy usually backfires. For example, on this particular my-wife-won't-let-me-take-a-nap day, our six-year-old, Jack, decided he was going to bring his harmonica to the park. A harmonica that his older sister, Marre, suddenly believed was hers. I had to then find the other harmonica so they both could lose the same thing at the park. Overhearing this conflict, three-year-old Katie insisted that she also wanted to bring a "moniker" to the park. Of course, there were only two harmonicas (aka monikers) so I had to convince Katie that a plastic red recorder was a fancy "moniker." Marre, ever supportive, seconded my lie. When my one-year-old, Michael, indicated in his unintelligible baby talk that he too wanted a "moniker," I just handed him a square baby pillow that made noise and informed him it was a harmonica. He seemed satisfied or just had gas.

As long as we are on the subject of gas, little kids have no awareness of if or when they need to use the bathroom. "Do you need to go to the bathroom? Do you think you may need to go to the bathroom? Why don't you just try to go to the bathroom?" They never need to go to the bathroom until you get to the place without a bathroom. I've become one of those parents who demand their children go to the bathroom.

"But I don't have to."

"Well, go anyway."

After everyone faked going to the potty, we were ready to go. Then Marre, being ever unsupportive, piped up, "Mom says we need sunscreen." My shoulders drooped as I grabbed the sunscreen and began the arduous process of protecting my pale offspring from the evil sun. I haven't even gotten out the door yet and I'm already exhausted. An hour later, we trekked down the five flights of stairs. I wore the newborn in a Björn, carried my one-year-old, and held the hand of my three-year-old while I pleaded with my six- and eight-year-olds to hold on to the railing. At the bottom I had the eight-year-old hold the hand of the one-year-old as I grabbed the double stroller off the second floor, where our childless neighbors had mercifully allowed us to store it with the big kids' scooters.

I pushed the one-year-old and the three-year-old in the double stroller as I wore the newborn and monitored the six- and eight-year-olds on their scooters. I was superdad. My relief at achieving departure from my apartment coupled with my utter exhaustion probably came across as confidence or calmness. Strangers looked at me like I was running a mobile day care. I proudly headed to the dog run. I mean playground. Because, unfortunately for a lazy guy like me, children, like dogs, need exercise and fresh air, and because we don't have a backyard, I can't just open the door and let them out. Well, I could, but I would probably get a visit from Children's Services.

Children need a backyard. This statement mostly comes

from friends who have moved to the suburbs in order to give their children a precious yard that they don't feel comfortable letting them play in because they've watched too much *Law & Order: Special Victims Unit*. I get the suburban yard argument, but given that I work in the city during the day and at night, I'd rather my children know me. I realize my children are missing something by not having a yard. A couple of years ago, my sister Cathy was living in a New York City suburb. We had Thanksgiving at her beautiful house with a spacious backyard. For months after that, my children kept requesting that we visit "the aunt with the house in the park."

New York City parks and playgrounds are really my children's backyard. Unfortunately, this means occasionally there are dead rats, homeless people, and used syringes in our backyard, but I think it gives my kids character and a strong immune system. So that's where we are headed today. Our backyard. And it only took us two hours to get there.

Going to the playground is never really a day at the park. Because my children are city kids who are growing up going to playgrounds, they sometimes complain about going to the same playground. "We went to that playground yesterday!" So we go to many playgrounds. New York City playgrounds are usually named after great New Yorkers who nobody has ever heard of. As a parent, you end up using nicknames to describe them. There's "Dirty Park" (DeSalvio Playground); "Injury Park" (Chinatown's Columbus Park); "Poser Park" (Bleecker Playground); "Kidnapper Paradise" (Ancient Playground); "First and First" (don't know actual name); "Heroin Addict Park" (Tompkins Square Park); and "The Park" (Central Park).

My kids' favorite part of a recent visit to Washington Square Park.

On more than one occasion, I've made excuses for the stumbling heroin addict. "Is that guy a zombie?"

"Actually, yes, he is." It is probably unique to NYC that your children can't play in a sandbox because it's closed due to rat poop.

The dynamics of New York City playgrounds are fascinating. There are typically children of every race and socioeconomic background. There are moms, dads, grandparents, and nannies. Some caretakers are on the phone, some are chatting with one another, and some are actually playing with their kids, but mostly the kids are on their own. Even though there are watchful eyes nearby, this is the place where children feel like they can run free. I love watching children socialize at the park. It is so much easier for young kids than it is for adults to make friends. The lines children use to introduce themselves with are fascinating.

"Do you like *Star Wars*? I like *Star Wars*."

To kid with a *Cars* T-shirt: "I've got that movie."

Or just a simple "Wanna play?"

Sometimes they won't say anything. They will just start playing with some kid they've never met. This would be the equivalent of going up to an adult that is dancing and just starting to dance with them. Yet when I tried that at the ballet, people assumed I was drunk. Granted, I was, but that's beside the point. If only all human interactions were as easy as they are for kids.

Sometimes my children will meet kids at the playground that are just jerks. I realize parents are supposed to let their children find their way in the world, and this includes dealing with bullies, but I can't help myself. If I sense a kid is not being polite, I'll interject myself into the situation.

"What's going on here?"

The other kid always looks at me like, "Oh, he's one of the crazy adults."

Once my then three-year-old son, Jack, approached some seven-year-olds playing cards at the park and just watched them. One of the boys looked at my son and said, "Go away. You're gross!" The other kids laughed.

I chimed in immediately. "No, *you're* gross! You are the grossest gross grosser in the world!" The bully ran with tears in his eyes to his caregiver, who glared at me. I just smiled in victory. I realize I won't always be there to defend my children, but if I can trim some of the jerky behavior out of their life, maybe they won't do it to other kids. Of course, I am also getting revenge for my own victimization as a child. I was always hoping some pale giant would appear and rescue me from the bullies. Now I am that pale giant. You shall call me Thor.

God help you if one of your kids has to use the bathroom. Remember, they didn't have to go at home, but (five minutes later) now they do. I've had some really difficult moments in my life, and using a New York City park bathroom with a three-year-old is up there. New York City park bathrooms feel like a crime scene. You are always expecting to see yellow police tape and a chalk-outlined body.

There's usually water running and a homeless man giving himself a sponge bath. He always looks at you like you broke into his house. The only thing about the New York City park bathroom that is unlike a crime scene is that crime scenes will eventually be cleaned up. You may ask me why—if it is so scary and disgusting and I am not a serial killer—would I ever use a New York City park bathroom? Why not go home, or to a nearby restaurant, or just buy my kid a new outfit? Anything but use a New York City park bathroom? I use it because when a three-year-old tells you they have to use the bathroom, she does not mean in a couple of minutes. She means at that moment. Actually, before that moment. They always tell you at the last possible moment.

THREE-YEAR-OLD: I need to use the bathroom.
ADULT: Now?
THREE-YEAR-OLD: Almost done.

Wet pants, a bad fall, and a temper tantrum are all signals that it is now time to leave the park. If you thought leaving your house with little kids was impossible, now there is the other crisis of returning home that must be dealt with. You could spend ten hours at the park, and your announcement

that it's time to leave will always be greeted with whines of
"Aw, man!" or "Five more minutes!" Of course, little kids
never want to leave anywhere. They never say, "You know,
I'm tired . . . let's head home." The more tired they get, the less
they want to leave, and the more necessary it becomes for you
to leave before the meltdowns start. To other people you are
never leaving at the correct time with your children. You're
either looked at strangely for leaving early—"You're going
already?"—or you're the irresponsible parent—"Your baby
seems really tired. Like he needs to go to bed." It's amazing
that people with kids ever go anywhere.

Suddenly, the only thing harder than leaving your house is
returning to your house. Even though it's an hour before dinner, you are forced to coax them out with the promise of ice
cream, the methadone of leaving the park. It works. Now to
clean them up and convince them to not tell Jeannie I got them
ice-cream cones. They always promise to not say a word, but as
we walk into the apartment, one will gleefully announce, "We
had ice-cream cones!"

"Oh, really? Did Daddy have one, too?"

"Of course I didn't."

"No! Daddy had a hot fudge sundae."

"What? I'm still going to eat dinner."

Is It Too Soon to Start Dating Again?

I often view other parents the way I view other comedians. I have great respect for them, but I always assume they are crazy. I'm usually right. My other assumption about parents who have children who are of a similar age to mine is that we will have something in common. I'm usually wrong.

"How old is your kid?" is the "How about this weather?" of parental playground talk. I am at the park to spend time with my kid, not to chat with some stranger, but the casual chat becomes inevitable. Talking to a parent I don't know at a playground can be an obstacle course. I try not to be too forward or too aloof. If the stranger parent is of the opposite sex, I don't want the banter to be considered flirtatious or otherwise creepy. If the conversation gets too serious and we start talking about an election, religion, or soy milk, it can get really weird. Therefore it always goes back to the safe option: asking the age of the stranger's child. Warning: Avoid guessing at a stranger parent's child's gender. You don't want to be wrong.

> ME: How old is he?
> STRANGER MOM: She's twenty-three years old!
> ME: Wow, lots of hair.

If this awkward chat goes on too long, and your kids like each other, you may get sucked into phase two of the interaction with the stranger parent: the awkward playdate. Given that I have enough kids for a basketball team, I rarely seek out playdates. I understand that other parents want to arrange playdates, and of course my kids love them. Playdates are great for kids and most often incredibly uncomfortable for me, given my general dislike of human beings.

Many times, playdates with parents I don't know feel like I am on a double date with my kid. My kid really likes his playdate friend and needs me as his wingman. He has set me up with someone I have no interest in hanging out with, but I'm doing him a solid. Suddenly I've traveled back in time to when I was single and trapped in that awful double-date scenario. I could always tell what my friends thought of me by the people they set me up with.

"What did you think of Lisa?"

"I'm not that desperate!"

For me, blind dates and first dates were nothing but awkwardness and discomfort. Playdates with a stranger parent are just déjà vu. "Oh, you guys don't eat meat or food?" "Yeah, I guess the park is dirty." "Tell me more about your job at the water filtration plant." I am forced to engage in endless empty parent talk while my kids live it up. To be fair, it's usually a great opportunity to discover that the only thing that I have in common with that parent is that we have a kid the same age.

Like a serial dater, I am spending time with strangers who I am not even on a first-name basis with. My phone is filled with numbers of people that I will probably never see again, and if I did, I would never know their real name: Milo's dad, Luca's mom, Silas's dad, Oliver's mom, that kid from Chelsea Piers' gay dad.

Rarely do I meet a parent at a park or on a playdate that I develop a lifelong friendship with. Someone should really start an online service for playdate matchups. Parents could take a personality test to see if they are compatible with other kids' parents before letting their kids become friends with kids with boring parents. It would narrow down the list of potential play-date partners' parents and help you avoid the inevitable walk of shame home from a horrible playdate. I would totally sign up for that service. I've got an idea. Why don't you start that business? You could call it "Playdates.com" or "ePlaydates.com." You could make a killing! You're welcome. Again. Don't tell me you don't have time. You're just sitting around reading this brilliant book. Me? No, thanks. I have five kids. Plus I don't like to work. Send me an e-mail when you have figured out your business plan. You can pay me then. I'll take 80 percent. All right, all right, 79 percent. Hey! It was my idea! Fine. I'll see you in court.

I'll Be Your Tour Guide

When you have five kids, or even more than one kid, it can be difficult to give everyone the appropriate amount of attention. Therefore I strive to get some quality one-on-one time with each of them. I'll proudly announce to Jeannie, "Michael [the one-year-old] and I are going to have some 'dad and son' time together this afternoon." Unfortunately, Jeannie will often say, "Fine, just don't take him somewhere to eat." I always think, "Then what are we supposed to do?" I mean, we could play catch, but he's not that great at catching, so it feels more like playing throw. I'll try to convince Jeannie that taking Michael to Katz's Deli could be a memory that he cherishes. I imagine adult Michael saying, "I remember when I was little, my dad would take me to Katz's for a pastrami sandwich. Occasionally, my dad would even let me have a bite. What a great dad I had." Yet Jeannie always insists on no food. She has this weird thing about eating large meals between meals. I know, she's a

Eating healthy at Katz's Deli. A tradition.

total weirdo, right? She also has this cockamamie notion that cured meat is not only bad for babies but bad for everyone! I call that "neglect."

When you only have one of your children with you, you have many more options of places to go in New York City besides parks or playgrounds (the only logical places you can safely bring the whole group). Here are my assessments of these nonfood places that are good for one-on-one bonding with a kid.

Children's Museums

I'm not really sure what makes a children's museum a museum. I guess just the word *museum*. Children's museums seem more like gathering places for toddlers to do fun activities while at the same time contracting a cold. I guess the idea is "Why have my kid ruin my house when he or she can go ruin this play area someone has named a museum?"

Regular Museums

NYC has some amazing regular museums that kids seem to enjoy. There's the Metropolitan Museum of Art, the Museum of Natural History, and a bunch of other ones I keep planning to take my children to. I know kids love these museums because whenever I take my kids to a NYC museum, they are way too crowded with other kids. Don't ever go to a museum on a rainy Saturday. It's like when the Walking Dead took over Atlanta. All right, I love *The Walking Dead.* Get used to me using it as a reference. Museums are a great cultural experience, and by that I mean a great opportunity for you to repeatedly tell your children not to touch things. I find museums incredibly exhausting, and by that I mean acting like you're interested in some of those exhibits. "So this is a painting by *another* European painter of another unattractive European from the 1700s? Fascinating." It seems like they were only painting the sad, ugly people back then. "Hey, you're hard on the eyes, why don't I paint your portrait?" To make matters worse, it's hard to leave a museum, mostly because you can never find the exit. I've been in casinos that are easier to navigate.

My head looks pretty big in this picture, right?

The Zoo

Kids love the zoo. I've been lucky enough to take my kids to many zoos across the United States. What I've learned is that when children see animals in captivity, it makes them want ice cream.

ME: Hey, there's a monkey!
KID: Can we get ice cream?

ME: Let's see the polar bear.
KID: After that can we get ice cream?
ME: Are you enjoying the animals?
KID: Do they have animal-shaped ice cream?

KrOcbILL

Movies

My kids love going to movies, and I enjoy taking naps during those movies. Sure, I'm not thrilled to pay twelve dollars to take a nap, yet it always seems worth it. I'm not even concerned that I'm missing the film, because I know I'll have another dozen times to see it at home when my kids watch it on Netflix or force me to buy it on iTunes for a thousand dollars.

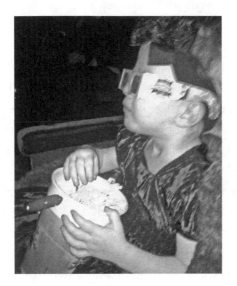

Movie + Popcorn = Dad can nap

Brooklyn Bridge

The grandeur of walking across the Brooklyn Bridge is a great activity that attracts many New Yorkers and tourists. The views are amazing, and it's free. Unfortunately, little kids are not big walkers. About one-third of the way across, they will start complaining that they want to "get off," and you will have to explain to them that this is not an attractive option. You keep them motivated by the great pizza place on the other side, but be prepared to take a forty-dollar cab ride back to Manhattan.

New York Yankees Game

A dad has to take his boy to a baseball game, right? Well, I didn't want my then three-year-old son, Jack, growing up and saying, "My dad never even took me to a baseball game." So we went. I picked up Jack at nursery school and took the long subway ride up to Yankee Stadium. I proudly announced to Jack that we were going to the ballpark. He seemed excited. I seemed excited. We arrived early and entered the stadium. I bought him a ten-dollar hot dog and we went to look for our seats. Suddenly Jack belted out, "Aw man!" What? What happened? How could he be disappointed already? The game hadn't even started! "Dad, this isn't a park! You said we were going to the park!" We struggled through three innings and three more ten-dollar hot dogs before we got the hell out of there. Dad-and-son Yankee game, check!

I don't mean to brag, but I dressed him that day.

Broadway Shows

Probably the most expensive thing you can do with your children in New York City is to take them to a Broadway show. We've seen *The Lion King, Mary Poppins, Shrek, Annie* (twice), and *Beauty and the Beast* (twice). The thing about having a bunch of kids is that you end up doing once-in-a-lifetime things more than once in a lifetime. Suddenly your new baby is four years old and that show is still on Broadway, and now *she* wants to see it. Sometimes the snacks at intermission cost you about as much as the overpriced ticket. I've yet to leave one of these shows and think, "Well that was worth the money."

Statue of Liberty

I'd lived in New York twenty years and still hadn't seen Lady Liberty in person. I'd had friends from out of town come and visit, and they would always want to take the ferry and see the statue. "No thanks, tell her I said hi." When they came back, my out-of-town friends would rave about the experience. Once I had children, I knew I had to take them to see what all the fuss was about.

One Saturday morning, I had the brilliant idea that it would be a perfect day to visit the Statue of Liberty. I wrangled our then three kids down to the South Ferry Station, where the Statue of Liberty ferry departs. When we arrived, it became apparent that ten zillion other people had the same brilliant idea. Realizing that my children were too young to notice a difference, we took the Staten Island Ferry instead. My children were just thrilled to get on a boat. I pointed as we passed the statue. "There she is, Lady Liberty!" I was a hero.

Empire State Building

(See Statue of Liberty but replace Staten Island Ferry with a taxicab.)

Through all of my visits to these great places, I have learned that the one thing they all have in common that makes any of them worthwhile is that you are there with your kid spending quality time. That's the most important thing: Quality time. The only other thing that could top the experience is quality time *and* a big pastrami sandwich. That would be *quality* quality time.

Pale Force

If you have no idea what I look like, I am a very pale person. My photo on the book cover was retouched to make the glare from my skin easier on your eyes. Hey, the publisher wanted to sell books. Trust me, I am a very pale person. No, I'm paler than that. Yes, *that* pale. Even when I look in the mirror, I think, "Wow, I'm pale!" I've never tanned. Growing up, I hated being pale. I was the whitest kid in an all-white community. Ironically, in a way I was the minority. As a kid, I was called "Whitey," "Casper," and "Albino." Other kids would ask, "Why are you sooooo pale?" I realize this is a minor form of bullying compared to what some have gone through, but to the ten-year-old me it was brutal. I felt like an outcast. I was the pale kid. I sometimes think that in addition to the influence of my father, I pursued being funny just to add an adjective before "pale." I would be the *funny* pale kid. So when I was asked, "Why is your hair sooooo white?" I'd respond,

"Because my father is a Q-tip." It got a laugh. It still hurt, but the laugh made it more bearable. Eventually I embraced my paleness. I even learned to laugh at my paleness. Now imagine five miniature versions of me, but not as dark skinned. During the summer, my children need sunscreen applied to them every ten minutes or they will die. I feel like I'm raising vampires. "Don't open the fridge, you'll kill yourself!"

Prior to having children, I never went outside. Well, I never went outside to *enjoy* the outdoors. I guess I'm what you would consider indoorsy. I didn't even know what a long-sleeve sun shirt was or how humiliating it is to wear one. Now I'm the proud owner of two long-sleeve sun shirts. One for formal swimming pools and one for casual swimming pools. Let me tell you, there is no boost to the ego quite like putting sunscreen on the top of your balding head, but I think swimming in a pool in a long-sleeve sun shirt is up there. Wearing a long-sleeve sun shirt in a swimming pool makes it impossible to not look like a moron. People always seem to look at me like I fell in.

"Is that guy just swimming in his clothes?"

"That's the worst suicide attempt I've ever seen."

I suppose our family paleness is entertaining to the outside world, but it adds another thick, white layer of difficulty to parenting that most people don't consider: sunscreen. Whoever decided that the protective goo that pale people need to slather liberally on their skin should be white and actually make them look paler is just cruel. But that's only the first problem with sunscreen. To fully grasp the commitment that sunscreen demands from me, consider the following. I hope this will be an easy book to read. If you wanted to, I suppose you could read this book in a few hours. That is roughly the time it takes to properly apply sunscreen to one of my children. Now multiply that by five. Now add in the fact that I have to sunscreen myself. Now you understand why I hate the summer. "We're going to the beach next week? Well, I'd better start putting sunscreen on them now." True, we are Catholic, but I sometimes feel that it's the sunscreen industry that is more pleased that Jeannie and I have so many children. We must be dramatically increasing overall sales.

It's not just the look, the cost, and the time involved in putting sunscreen on a child, it's the battle. My kids have no idea why they would have to wait to have fun while they are smeared with chemicals all over their face and body. They scream. They cry. "It burns!" The process of applying sunscreen just highlights the preposterousness of raising pale kids on a planet that revolves around a hot burning star that emits poisonous UV rays. I can never tell if the concerned looks from strangers are because they think I am torturing my children or because I am dressed like an out-of-shape Superman at the beach. Does anyone know where I can get a red swim cape?

For some reason those bastards at Sports Illustrated *didn't think this was "cover worthy" for their swimsuit issue.*

Learnin' Them

Newborns arrive as a blank slate, a tabula rasa, or as I call them, dummies. Every parent must start from scratch and teach them everything. Kids have a whole lot of learning to do. Of course, not from me, because I also am a dummy. The apple doesn't fall far from that thing it grows on. Luckily there are classes, activities, and, of course, school.

I really wasn't prepared for the amount of classes offered to little children. When I was a kid, there was only preschool and watching television. Now, the moment after conception, there are classes specifically geared toward your fetus. For example, there is prenatal yoga. It's a lot like a regular yoga, but it has the word *prenatal* before it.

Once your child is born, the "classes" for one- and two-year-olds run the gamut from pointless to useless. You are essentially paying an enormous amount of money to take your baby to some room in order to interact with them. Parents sit in a circle on the floor and sing horrible songs led by some well-intended struggling musician as the two-year-olds run around the room screaming and try to hit each other with the musical instruments that have been handed out. Toddler classes are no better. Toddler soccer is like watching a political discussion on cable news. It starts off serious and ends in embarrassment for all involved. "Waaaaah, he stole my ball!" Yeah, Jack, that's the point of the game.

Luckily, as your child gets older, the good people that run these classes continue to take advantage of parental enthusiasm and guilt. When she was six, my daughter Marre was in a dance class that ended with a performance that parents had to pay $35 to get into. That's right. I had to pay to see my six-year-old twirl around the stage for five minutes dancing a routine she learned in a class I paid for her to attend. The experience was made complete when I opened a fundraising letter from the "school" the next week.

Eventually children start actual school. When I was single, I never understood those commercials with the parents celebrating the end of summer. Now I understand that around mid-August, all the summer camps are over and you've run out of constructive things to do with your kid and you are desperate to get them out of the house. You've grown tired of your four-year-old pointing to words and asking, "What does this say?" Apparently it's not okay to respond to them with, "It says, 'Learn how to read.'" You don't want to get rid of your children, but you do want to get rid of them for a couple of hours a day.

School seems like a perfect solution. Your precious child will learn something, and most important, you will be able to use the bathroom in peace. My only problem with school is when it starts and ends. Preschool boils down to a couple of hours a day for you to run errands. Elementary school starts at the ungodly hour of 8 a.m. Yes, in the morning. Given that a first grader can't put on a T-shirt properly, they will need help at the even ungodlier hour of 7 *a.m.* Since I decided to raise an entire basketball team that can barely dress themselves, I have to wake up, too.

It's not just getting them to schools, it's what they can and cannot bring with them. When I first moved to New York City, I remember hearing stories of little children bringing guns to elementary school. Thankfully this trend is over, but it has been replaced by little children bringing far more dangerous weapons to school, such as the peanut butter sandwich. During the first weeks of school there are e-mails and e-mail reminders instructing parents that children are forbidden to bring anything containing nuts into the school. I realize a nut allergy is no joke, but I can't think of one child growing up that had a nut allergy. Now they are more common than Velcro sneakers. Today it seems every other child has a nut allergy. Sometimes I think, "Why don't they just open a school for children without nut allergies?" I'm all for small class size.

There was one paranoid teacher at our nursery school that would check the children's backpacks as they came in to make sure no one smuggled in anything produced in a facility that may have possibly also produced something containing a trace of nuts or something that sounded like nuts. That sounds nuts, right? I was less shocked that they were checking the backpacks than I was shocked that nursery students *had* backpacks. Why a three-year-old would need a backpack is beyond me, but my daughter Katie has one, too. She has nothing in there. She'll wear her backpack for a couple of minutes and then hand it off to me to carry up the stairs to her classroom. She has a kid in her class who has a backpack with wheels on it. Yes, wheels. That way, when the child gets tired of carrying the things they don't need to nursery school, they can roll the bag of nothing around. Perfect.

I love the preschools that my children have attended, but they are not really "schools," and this applies to all of them. No matter whether they are called a Preschool, a Nursery, or an Early Learning Center, they are either just a day care or a jail. That's why I find it strange that they still hold parent-teacher conferences. The preschool parent-teacher conference always feels like a game of "serial killer or not serial killer?" You either find out your child is dismembering dolls or not dismembering dolls. This is not to say you don't learn insightful things about your child: "Your daughter likes to sing and loves the color green." Or see their artwork: "This is what your daughter scribbled last week. And this is what she scribbled this week." Of course, you want to hear your kid is doing well and getting along with the other children, but unless your child is building bombs or purposely urinating in the Quiet Corner, the parent-teacher conference for a nursery student is incredibly pointless and could easily be done over e-mail.

Even as your children get older, the parent-teacher conference is always a strange experience. The conference is supposed to be all about the child, but somehow it ends up with you feeling like you are getting a report card on your parenting. You still want to know your child is doing well and you still

want to see their work, but because I am an actor and comedian, it seems that these conferences always lead back to my
occupation. "Well your daughter/son is very *dramatic* and loves
to *talk*, which I guess is no surprise, given your occupation."
I'm not offended, but the implication that all improper behavior is the result of what I do for a living is rather absurd. As if a
chatty five-year-old with a librarian mom would be a red flag.
"We expected your child to just sit behind her desk and shush
people. Maybe she needs Ritalin."

Do you think they're too little for school?

A Self-Portrait

Sometimes I feel I could spend my whole day dropping off and picking up my children, and, frankly, I do. No, really I do. I'm writing this right now on the subway after I dropped off my daughters at school. I tell you, some of the looks you get on the New York City subway. People act like they've never seen a typewriter before. This time-sucking parenting task is made even more complicated in New York City without a car. My kids are really going to be surprised to find out I'm charging them for all these back and forths.

I belong in NYC, but I don't fit in NYC. I've lived in NYC for over twenty years, and I'm still treated like a tourist. I've had more than one cab driver ask me, "Where are you visiting from?" I always sense they are trying to take advantage of "the tourist." I could be going five blocks, and I'll have cab drivers ask if I'd like "to take the George Washington Bridge?" Yes, can we also swing by LaGuardia Airport and pick up some groceries since I'm naive because I have blond hair? I've lived in NYC long enough to forget how truly white bread I look. Occasionally I'll be on the subway and I'll see some tourists from Iowa, and I'll think to myself, "Ha ha! Check out those people. . . . Oh wait, that's exactly what I look like."

At this point, I'm comfortable not really fitting in anywhere in New York City. I'm not a hipster, I'm not a Wall Street guy, I'm not one of the fashionable, and I'm not even one of the antifashionable fashionables. I feel most comfortable among the homeless and the oddball characters on the Bowery. Of course, having our children going to schools near the Bowery would be too easy.

One year, we had two babies at home and two children at two different schools. Wait, it gets better. These two schools were in completely different parts of the city, and each provided their own special form of awkwardness for me. Marre was and is attending a fancy all-girls Catholic school on the Upper East Side. The school building is a former Vanderbilt mansion. Think *Madeline* and roughly as far away from our home on the Bowery as, well, as Paris, France, is from the Bowery. The school is a warm, amazing place populated by the daughters of the titans of finance and industry. The girls wear adorable light-blue uniforms and actually "stand in two straight lines." When I go for drop-off or pickup, I'm usually the only parent in jeans wearing a baseball cap. I probably look unshowered because often I am. The other parents are very nice, but I usually feel that for some reason I'm being treated as the strange Downtowner who tells jokes for a living. Oh, wait, I guess I am.

Our second-oldest, Jack, was attending an amazing "play-based" preschool in the East Village. I still don't exactly know what "play-based" means, but I just remember the classroom not having any chairs and me being one of the only parents without a tattoo or a child named after a spice. Housed in a turn-of-the-century brownstone, the school felt a little like the beacon to nineteenth-century street kids it once was. The other parents were very nice, but for some reason I usually felt like I was being treated as the strange white-bread guy who tells jokes for a living. Oh, wait, I guess I am.

Given I'm more of an afternoon guy than a morning guy. I often do the pickup portion of the round-trip. I would usually get Jack first in the East Village, then make the trek to the Upper East Side to get Marre. Every afternoon, I would enter the basement / locker-room area / greeting area of Jack's school and check out the artwork the children had made hang-

Some "art" from "school."

ing on the walls while I waited. It always feels a little generous calling a preschool's artwork "artwork."

One afternoon I was looking at the "self-portraits" of the Pre-K class drawn on yellow construction paper. In one hand-crafted picture, there was a toilet paper roll jutting out of the top area of the legs. I chuckled to an ironic T-shirted, fedora-wearing father, "That looks like a penis." The father looked at me like I had just cut PBS funding, "What's wrong with that?" I don't know, everything?

At that point, Jack arrived with his teacher.

TEACHER: Oh, you saw Jack's artwork.

ME: [*Beat.*] I did.

JACK: It's my penis.

ME: I recognized it.

TEACHER: We encourage the kids to express themselves about their bodies without any shame or guilt.

ME: Good, good.

TEACHER: You're welcome to take it home.

ME: Oh, I can't wait to show Jack's mom.

As we taxied up to the Upper East Side, Jack held his penis artwork on his lap and told me about his day. Well, actually, I asked him about his day, and he said he didn't remember anything.

At Marre's school, we waited with the other moms for dismissal in the grand lobby of the former mansion. Often pickups at Marre's school feel like I'm just conducting a press conference for Jeannie while stopping Jack from climbing on the grand staircase.

MOM #1: Where's Jeannie?

MOM #2: How's Jeannie?

MOM #3: Why aren't you Jeannie?

While fielding questions from the mom press on that particular day, I turned and saw the head of Marre's school greeting Jack.

MS. ALVAR: How are you, Jack?

JACK: Great! Wanna see my penis?

Two pickups, two sides of town, two equal doses of awkward. I scurried my children out the mansion doors onto Fifth Avenue and into a cab.

A half hour later we arrive in front of our building on the Bowery. I give Marre and Jack each a quarter so they can get a gumball from the gumball machine outside of Patricia Field's boutique (the gumball machine conveniently located between two mannequins in full S&M garb). As I wait for the kids, my friend the six-foot bearded drag queen André greets me.

"Hey, Jim."

"Hey, André."

There's no place like home.

Your Special Day

When you have a child, a really fun thing to do is to throw them birthday parties. The first baby's first birthday is an unforgettable event. Normally, during the first year of your first baby's life, you and your wife will not go out and party like you used to. Ever. You are busy being consumed with figuring out the new-baby thing, and you really don't feel comfortable leaving the baby with anyone else. You barely see your friends during that first baby's first year, so by the time the first birthday rolls around, you are really ready for a party. The first baby's first birthday party is not a party for your baby; it's a party for you. Sure, the baby will someday appreciate that photo of them in front of the cake with the "1" candle and the photo of them taking their first bite of cake, but when a baby turns twelve months old, they really have no idea that they are even at a party, or that the party is actually for them, because their entire life seems like a party. A party for them. Everything is always new and exciting, they are always the center of attention, and, to them, most people look like clowns anyway. Except for the photos, it really doesn't matter if a baby is even *at* their first birthday party. They wouldn't even notice if you didn't throw them a party at all. You are the one that needs the party. The baby obviously has no friends yet, so the guest list is all your friends you haven't seen for a year. And since your friends are the guests, they will obviously need good food, good drinks, and music, and suddenly you have the recipe for a raging bash and you take the pictures of your baby in front of the cake, put them to bed, and carry on like, well, like you don't have a baby.

Even after that first baby's first birthday party, you still love throwing your kids birthday parties. You remember how exciting your own birthday parties were as a kid, even if it was just your mom taking you and a few friends to that disgusting McDonald's indoor playground, it was still the time of your life. You want your kid to have that experience, too, so you throw them a fun birthday party. And guess what? All the evil, greedy businesses out there *know* you want to do it, and they see it as a wonderful way to take advantage of your desire to rekindle your childhood memories and throw your kids a fun birthday party by robbing you blind. You will soon find out that every chain restaurant, children's museum, skate rink, bowling alley, toy store, and gymnastics club will offer "Birthday Party Packages" to save you the trouble of having all the kids over to your place for the small fee of a hundred billion dollars. A small price to pay for all the cheap, plastic, toxic made-in-China, unnecessary gifts that the other kids' parents picked up on the way to the party that you are just going to end up regifting when your kid gets invited to one of their friends' parties.

If your own kid's birthday parties are fun, double that on

how unfun other people's kids' birthday parties are. Because most two- to six-year-olds don't drive or even know their own address, an adult will most likely also have to attend other kids' parties with them. Given that my family has roughly the same population as South Dakota, I've already been to too many other kids' birthday parties.

Other people's children's birthday parties are the most joyful events you will ever resent having to attend. The reality of the sheer quantity of birthday parties you will be attending kicks in around kindergarten. It will seem like every kid in your children's class has a birthday at least once a year. Can you believe that? Birthday parties trickle in and take over like an infestation of termites eating away at your Saturdays. They are in strange locations and at inconvenient times. My daughter Marre was invited to a birthday party that started at 9 a.m. on Saturday. Yes, 9 a.m. means morning, and Saturday means weekend. I actually thought it was a joke at first. I found myself asking Marre questions like "How good of a friend are you with this strange Audrey girl?" "Wouldn't you rather watch cartoons on Saturday morning?" "How much would someone have to pay you to not go to this party?" I was ready to tell Marre that Saturday parties before noon were against our religion until Jeannie agreed to go.

Attending a birthday party for a little kid can be pretty awkward, especially if you weren't invited. Sometimes you aren't invited, just your child is. These parties are called "drop-offs," where you leave your children in the care of some frazzled strangers at a Build-A-Bear Workshop, and you walk off with just enough time to do nothing except be that creepy guy wandering around a mall with a diet Coke being tailed by a suspicious security guard until you have to pick up your face-painted, sugar-highed puddle of a child.

Even if you only have one or two kids, by the time they are in grade school, you will have brought them to so many birthday parties it will become somewhat of a routine. After coaxing your child into crafting something resembling a card and taping it onto that poorly wrapped, regifted present from their own birthday party, you rush the overexcited kid wearing their favorite outfit out the door, and you are on your way to the party. Then you realize that you forgot the regift, so you run back to get it, and now you are late and your kid is furious at you because they feel they have now missed "the funnest part." Upon arrival at the venue, your child runs away immediately, and you are left awkwardly holding your embarrassing present, praying that it was not originally from the kid whose birthday party it is, making small talk with parents you barely know, and trying to get through the conversation without revealing that you totally forgot their name and you don't know who their kid is. After some games no one wants to participate in, some ugly, glue-dribbled craft your kid makes that you plan on tossing into the first dumpster you see on the way home, and the inevitable pizza, it's time for the cake. The cake is the fat lady singing of the little-kid birthday party. The final act. The climax of the birthday party. What everyone has been waiting for. Kids love cake, and who can blame them.

Everyone loves cake, but at the other kid's birthday party you also love cake for what it represents. The end. The time to go home. You are officially excused to leave the birthday party after the cake. It's the last hymn at church. Sometimes the much-anticipated exit takes a little longer because the cake has ice cream to go with it. I'm always amazed how we serve ice cream with cake at a little kid's birthday party. "Hey, you, what would be really good with this sugar bread? Some frozen sugar milk. Now let's give it to the four-year-olds and see how they respond. Sugar doesn't affect children, right? We are about to hand them back to the care of their parents, anyway." And just as you are exiting the party with your tearful, screaming, prediabetic child over your shoulder, you are handed exactly what you need for the way home. The treat bag filled with candy. I am pretty sure this is the formula that was used to prepare the young Linda Blair for filming the bed scene in *The Exorcist.*

Ice cream makes kids so happy.

Losing My Religion

Anyone who has ever taken their babies and kids to a church, a temple, a mosque, a wedding, a funeral, or any other place of reverence understands the true meaning of torture.

Obviously I am against torture, yet I still take my kids to church.

The question remains, who am I really torturing? Am I torturing myself, because it's virtually impossible to get a young child to sit still and listen to some old guy go on and on about metaphors they don't understand? Am I torturing my children, because church is the opposite of a video game? Am I torturing the innocent churchgoers sitting around me trying to listen and being distracted by my kids climbing on the pews or playing peek-a-boo with them?

The answer is "All of the Above."

Cast photo: Baptism no. 5

I empathize with my children. If you've never been to a Catholic Mass, don't worry, it's still going on, you still have time to catch it. I remember when I was a kid, I really thought that church was eight hours long. At times it felt like they were dragging church out on purpose. "Aaaaahhhhh-meeeeeen." I remember thinking, "Amen, already. Let's wrap it up, Padre. I got some sinning to do." It was too early, too boring, smelled weird, and was filled with the oldest people on the planet. "How did you get here? What was Jesus like as a kid?" I used to have to do readings in church, and it was terrifying. I would never have my glasses. The words are printed so small even Superman would be nervous. And you're reading from the Bible. It's not like you can just make something up and improvise. "A reading from the letter of Saint Paul to the Corinthians. Uhhh. Dear Corinthians, ... How was your weekend? Sure is hot here. Uh, tell Jesus 'Hey.' This is the word of the Lord."

When I was growing up, just getting to church caused such anxiety in our home, it seemed to defeat the purpose. Sunday mornings, my dad would bark, "Hurry up or we're going to be late for church, God dammit!" At that age, church to me was all about strict obedience, uncomfortable clothes, and memorization. I remember my father glaring at me during Mass to see if I knew my prayers.

Even now I find myself dreading going to Mass. It's not just the battle with the kids. God really should have talked to the NFL before deciding to put church on Sunday. Family church on Sunday is all Jeannie's idea. Even if there is no way my kids can figure out what's going on in there, Jeannie insists that the routine and the exposure to it will someday benefit them. Jeannie is very Catholic. She is like a Shiite Catholic. She's already received her early admission to heaven.

I can never get Jeannie to leave church after Mass. "Why don't we stay and talk to the weirdest people here?" There are definitely some serious crazies at church. Whenever I meet a real nut job at church, I am always grateful that they are going to church. Imagine how crazy they would be if they didn't have rules to follow.

Yes, I take my five children to church because I, too, am one of those crazies. Kids are way too noisy for church, and everyone reminds you of that while your children are acting up by turning their head around to look at you. This in turn makes everyone else turn their head around to look at you. As if looking at you is somehow going to make your kids behave instead of just making you feel horrible. No matter how much talking or singing there is at church, kids always find that brief moment of silence to make a loud announcement. "Michael did a poop in his diaper!" Also, if you take your kid to the bathroom at church one time, every time you take them to church, they will constantly tell you they have to go to the bathroom. They don't need to go to the bathroom, they just need a break from church. And they know you have to take them. They know you live in fear of saying no because that one time you do say no will be the one time they actually do need to go to the bathroom, and then you will really be up that creek you can't talk about in church. So you continue to take them to the bathroom, and deep down you don't mind, because you also need a break from church.

This is an actual photo from the Bible. No, really.

Then there is the spectacle of carrying your misbehaving child out of church and taking them to the back until they quiet down. This is another dilemma, because taking them to the back is actually a reward for them, and it just encourages them to misbehave more often.

I don't want them to view church as a punishment. I do see the value in routine, tradition, and family time. I have tried to give them positive associations with going to church by offering the kids a treat after church as an incentive to behave: "If you are good in church, we will go out for pancakes." This also backfires, because once you mention pancakes, that's all they are going to think about and therefore talk about during the entirety of the church service. "Is it time for pancakes yet? Can I have syrup on my pancakes? Are there chocolate chip pancakes?" [*To a parishioner:*] "We are going for PANCAKES!"

There is no way your small child is going to have a spiritual experience at church. The only times I have ever had a spiritual experience at church are when my kids were *not* at church. I think I may have heard the voice of God say, "Thanks for not bringing your kids to church."

No Such Thing
as a Free Babysitter

When you first have a baby, it seems like all your friends, siblings, and even sometimes strangers want to help. "Hey, if you ever need someone to babysit, let me know." It actually appears as if everyone is begging to watch your kids. What a relief! It takes a village, right? A very short time later, you will realize that, in reality, no one wants to babysit or even help at all. They just want to say they offered. *Offering* is the kind gesture. Fine. Whatever. I don't need your help anyway. Besides, I wouldn't want some weirdo or relative watching my new baby. I am the parent, and I am not looking to outsource, thank you. I am an American, buddy!

Eventually the need for a babysitter creeps in as sneakily as reality TV took over and ruined prime time. Inevitably you are forced to give up the naive belief that you will be with your child every moment of their life. You need help. The question is, who should watch your angel? Who could ever be worthy of the all-important task of sitting in your apartment while your child sleeps?

The go-to is your parents. You know they are not serial killers. They want to see their grandchild, and you don't want to pay anyone. The perfect situation! The problem is, when you are not paying someone to do a favor for you, they don't really need to listen to you. "No candy" means "Your heartless parents don't give you candy, so I will give you tons of candy so you will like me better than your parents." Also your mom and dad are crazy. They raised you, and you are a disaster! By letting them watch your kids, you are giving them free rein to replicate their mistakes. To make matters worse, by the time your parents are grandparents, they are not equipped to deal with children. I know my parents wouldn't be good at babysitting, mostly because they've been dead for a decade. Actually they might be better at it now. Do less damage.

Initially letting someone that is not you or your spouse watch your child is nerve-racking. You check in, remind them to pay attention, and eventually you cut your obligation short to race home to your newborn. The free babysitters are brief. You go through your parents, your siblings, and the rare friend who is not an alcoholic. You then must hire some stranger to watch your prized possessions and also your kids. See what I did there? Kind of funny, right? Well, I thought it was.

Choosing a babysitter that is not a family member is one of the real struggles of parenting. Who to hire? Are they attentive? Do they have a criminal record? Eventually you become more lax in your approach. "Do you have a pulse? We'll be home around ten."

Of course, I'm joking. Kind of. With more children comes a greater need for help. As you add more and more children to the mix, the price goes up as the babysitting pool diminishes and you become more efficient at selecting a babysitter. For instance, the necessity of speaking English shrinks dramatically. The following is an actual conversation I had with a babysitter.

JEANNIE: Jim, this is Zanga.

JIM: [*Shaking hands.*] Nice to meet you. Where are you from?

ZANGA: Yes.

JIM: What country are you from?

ZANGA: Yes.

JEANNIE: She's from Sri Lanka.

JIM: Oh, Sri Lanka. That's where the Tamil Tigers are from, right?

ZANGA: Yes. Tsunami. Very sad.

JIM: Well, thanks for helping us out, Zanga.

ZANGA: Very sad.

JIM: Very sad.

I wish I was exaggerating. We once had a non-English-speaking babysitter from Guatemala who I'm pretty sure didn't even speak Spanish. Someone who doesn't know English shouldn't be watching my children, you say? In any small business, like parenting five children, it is necessary that you place the right people where their assets can be most useful in order to run a successful operation. Sometimes all the training a babysitter needs is having been a good mother herself. I don't care if some early childhood education grad student has taken twelve infant CPR classes, it will never replace the experience of a sitter who has raised her own well-adjusted children. No English is required for this position.

Let me familiarize you with some of my other categories of babysitters.

The Warm Body

I never said these categories would be flattering. When you have five kids, it's completely necessary to have a warm body to sit at your house while you are gone for a short while. When children are asleep, we have no problem leaving them with the Warm Body sitting in our living room while we go out and do shows in Manhattan for a couple of hours. They are literally a baby-sitter. Well, when they are not going through our stuff.

The College Student

This type of sitter is ideal for pickups and drop-offs because they know the NYC subway system, and your kids think they are some cool aunt from the Disney Channel. However, if you try to leave them with your kids at night, be prepared to pay eighteen dollars an hour for someone who will be texting their boyfriend constantly, and your computer history will show that they were checking in on Facebook more often than checking in on your kids. You will likely come home to an empty fridge and a sink full of dishes, and they will ditch you for the first unpaid NYU student film they can book.

The Manny

Initially I was hesitant to have another man babysit my kids. What if he is better with my kids than I am? What if he is worse with my kids than I am? I've grown to love it. It's really awesome to have a guy watch your kids. He can carry the stroller and a kid up five flights with no complaint and will keep them outside and active all day. You will not care at all that he does not clean or organize the diaper bag, because after all, he's a dude! Just the fact that he is a guy that can stand to be around other people's kids is amazing to me.

The Mary Poppins

It was love at first sight when you saw this babysitter interacting with other kids at the park. You immediately poached her from the family she was working for by offering her more money. This babysitter does it all. She's warm and reads stories and plays dress-up and cooks and cleans and is part teacher, part best friend. She knows all the names of the different X-Men. Your kids love her, and she will eventually get poached by a richer family at the park. Karma. Note: If you met your wife while she was married to another man, history is bound to repeat itself.

The Blackmailer

This babysitter will be amazing at first, and you will keep increasing her responsibilities. You will become completely dependent on her, and she will be an integral part of your daily routine and schedule. Inevitably, she will get involved in gossiping with the other sitters at the park and find out that someone makes more money for fewer kids or gets a MetroCard or federal holidays off (when there is no school and you need someone the most). Then when you have your busiest week with your most important deadline, she will threaten to quit unless she immediately receives all the aforementioned perks, and you are forced to give in to all of her demands. Of course, she will always hold one of the demands back and save it for the next time you are in a position of weakness.

The Attention Seeker

This babysitter will always be going through some personal crisis and make you feel as if you somehow had something to do with it. They will interrupt you during a business phone call to inform you that they found some mess that your kids made instead of just cleaning it up. They will create drama with any other babysitter that you hire to fill in when you need someone extra. The Attention Seeker will have some really positive attributes to justify you keeping her around, but eventually it becomes too much to bear, because your kids are also attention seekers and there is not enough attention to go around as it is.

———

The irony of the babysitting situation is that you need someone to watch your kids while you go out to earn the money
to pay someone to take care of your kids. Your ultimate goal
by earning the money is to be able to spend quality time with
your kids, which is what you are paying your babysitter to do.
The babysitting thing is my own personal Sisyphus story of
endlessly rolling the rock up the hill and watching it roll back
down. It's actually your fault, really, because you made me
write this book so you could read it. How selfish of you!

How to Put Five Kids to Bed in a Two-Bedroom Apartment

Living in a tiny two-bedroom apartment with five children makes bedtime a logistical nightmare. We have two single beds in the kids' room and one king in our master bedroom. No, these aren't big rooms. Think breadbox, but smaller. There is a crib in each of these rooms and also a crib on prominent display in the middle of our living room / office / dining room / kitchen because we love to show off our crib. (Pun intended.) We have three cribs. We have so many cribs, we should be on that show *Cribs*. Or at least in pun jail.

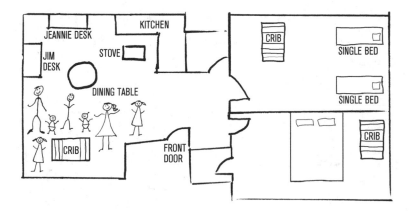

Given the number of children we have, bedtime must occur in waves. Babies (newborn and one-year-old) are placed in cribs, one in the kids' room and one in the master.

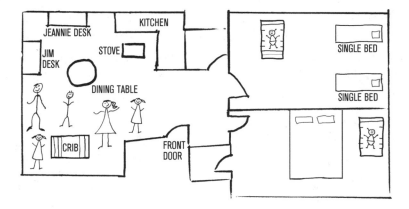

Then the hard part commences: the coordinating of teeth-brushing and using the bathroom with the big three. Once teeth are cleaned and everyone uses the potty, there is cuddling and stories with the big three, and then, out of necessity, the most raucous one is temporarily placed in our bed in the master, which has now become the "holding cell." If you are keeping track at home, we have three kids in one room and two in the other.

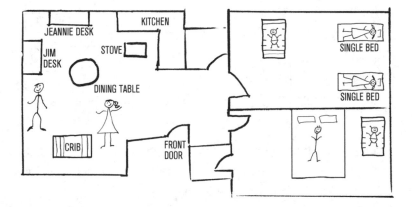

Now you may be wondering, why don't we have bunk beds? We learned with our first two kids that bunk beds are great except when a two-year-old crawls up to the top bunk, jumps, and falls on her face. We finally got rid of the bunk beds when we started to be on a first-name basis with the receptionist at the ER. Back to the present scenario. After the kids are in their secure location, I will run out and do a show or two. Jeannie will do whatever she does to hold our lives together. This part of the evening is known as a quasi "intermission." After I come back, Act II begins. Jeannie and I will do work, write, and try to maintain some semblance of a grown-up relationship. This all takes place in the living room, where there are no kids.

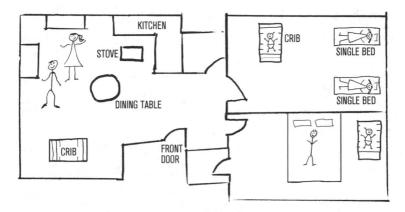

As you can see, we have made optimal use of the apartment. We have all the children snug in each of our beds. You may wonder where Jeannie and I sleep, since all the beds are occupied. This could be a major conflict. Begin Act III. If Jeannie and I plan to read or watch television in bed (which is every night, by the way), then a "transfer" must occur. The child that is in our bed must be moved into one of the singles with one of the other kids. Then the baby that is in our room must be moved from the crib in our room to the crib that is in the now quiet and dark living room / dining room / office / kitchen.

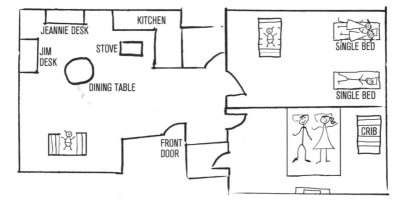

Then Jeannie and I can watch television or read for exactly one minute before they all wake up and come into our bed. Curtain.

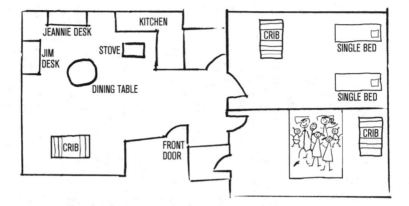

So how do we have time to *make* all these babies, you might ask? Well, that's none of your business, you pervert. Why don't you go reread that dirty book with the tie on the cover? I can't believe you read that stuff! Scandalous! I'm sorry. Maybe I'm overreacting. I'm grateful you bought my nondirty book. You obviously are a good person . . . with some naughty secrets. I won't hold your creepiness against you.

Negotiating with Terrorists

Exactly one million years ago, there was a television show called *The Waltons*. Each episode of *The Waltons* would end with an exterior shot of the Waltons' home at nighttime. The camera would hold on the house as the family said their round robin of goodnights as the light in the windows went out. Each person in the family would chime in. "Goodnight, Mama; goodnight, Daddy." "Goodnight, Jim-Bob; goodnight, John-Boy." This would go on for about a minute. It was adorable; it was sweet and probably the most unrealistic portrayal of bedtime for parents ever displayed in any art form.

Of course *bedtime* is a misleading term. It should be categorized with the word *utopia*. "Bed*time*" gives the impression that your children will be in bed, going to sleep at a specific *time*. Any parent of a five-year-old will tell you this is not a plausible reality. Bedtime with young children is a nightly crisis. Part of me is relieved that most of my shows coincide with bedtime, and therefore I have a valid excuse to remove myself from this catastrophic paradox.

Bedtime makes you realize how completely incapable you are of being in charge of another human being. My children act like they've never been to sleep before. "Bed? What's that? No, I'm not doing that." They never want to go to bed. This is another thing that I will never have in common with my children. Every morning when I wake up, my first thought is, "When can I come back here?" It's the carrot that keeps me motivated. Sometimes going to bed feels like the highlight of my day.

Ironically, to my children, bedtime is a punishment that violates their basic rights as human beings. Once the lights are out, you can expect at least an hour of inmates clanging their tin cups on the cell bars. They turn against us in a unified protest as fervent as the civil rights marches of the 1960s. "This is unfair!" Before the pajama burning begins, we move quickly into action following the "divide and conquer" strategy.

Part of our bedtime ritual involves Jeannie and I lying down with our kids. We'll cuddle them, read to them, tell them stories, and eventually beg them to sleep. This strategy always begins as a wonderful, intimate experience and then ends with threats and tears. And sometimes the kids get upset, too. Inevitably it becomes a hostage negotiation, but in reverse. "If you *stay in* there, we will give you whatever you want. What do you need, a helicopter to Cuba? We will meet all of your demands if you *just stay in there and don't hurt anyone!*"

With five little kids, there is no ending to bedtime. There is always one awake. Like they are taking shifts. I imagine they have scheduling meetings: "All right, I'll annoy Dad from midnight to two. Who wants the three-to-six-a.m. shift? Now everyone lie down and practice kicking Dad in your sleep." Whenever one of my children says, "Goodnight, Daddy," I always think to myself, "You don't mean that."

My Former Bed

I love my bed. It was a big investment. It's a Tempur-Pedic. You may have seen one of their annoying commercials on television where overly excited Tempur-Pedic owners make the appeal "Ask me about my Tempur-Pedic!" "Ask me how fast I fall asleep!" I always want to chime in, "Ask me why my Tempur-Pedic is filled with a horde of children every morning and I'm so uncomfortable."

This is because my bed, our bed, is a "family bed." There are two philosophies when it comes to getting young children to sleep. There is "sleep training," which basically involves putting your kids to bed and listening to them scream all night, or there is "attachment parenting," which essentially involves lying down with your kids, cuddling them, and then listening to them scream all night. The family bed is an additional aspect of attachment parenting.

Since Jeannie is a big believer in attachment parenting and I'm a spineless coward, we have instituted an open-door policy, meaning if one of our kids has a nightmare, they are welcome to come in our room and pee in our bed. Luckily this only happens every night.

I don't know if you have ever slept next to someone that has wet the bed, but it's delightful. You're asleep, right? So when you wake up, your first thought is, "Oh my God, I wet the bed!" For me, my next thought is, "Well, it's not *that* wet. I'll just scoot over a bit. If I act like I'm sleeping, maybe Jeannie will change the sheets." Some of my finest acting has been pretending to be asleep while Jeannie cleans up the mess. I'll groggily comment, "Oh, I didn't notice that. Hey, while you're up, can you make me a sandwich?"

Sometimes I'm awake when one of my kids will stumble into my room. I'll be innocently watching TV when I'll catch a shadowy figure in our bedroom doorway out of the corner of my eye. It always scares the hell out of me. They'll just be standing there blankly staring like they should be holding a knife. After I ask if they are okay, they'll climb in our bed and proceed to complain that I have the TV on.

"Turn off the TV!" my six-year-old son, Jack, will whine. Like I'm interrupting him.

"Why don't you just go back to your own bed?"

"Dad, turn off the TV—I am TRYING TO SLEEP!"

He's mostly upset because I'm watching the news. TV news is like kryptonite to children. The two major shifts in taste from childhood to adulthood are news and mustard. Kids hate the news and mustard. Hell, mustard even has the word *turd* in it. Maybe I should threaten my kids that if they don't go to bed, I will force them to watch an hour-long newscast about mustard.

I love the fact that if my children wake up scared or are feeling lonely, they can come in our bed. I just wish each and every one of them didn't do it every single night. There isn't room. I'm not exaggerating. There are seven people in my family, and there has yet to be a bed created in which we can all comfortably fit. I have a king-size bed, yet my dominion is relegated to the sliver on the right edge. One more peasant revolt and I'll be on the floor. By the end of the night, I find myself longing for my own cot. It could be made of nails, but it would be my own.

I blame Dr. Sears, the advocate of "attachment parenting," for this. Obviously I love all the intentions of attachment parenting, but often attachment parenting seems to just be a synonym for "Dad will be uncomfortable" parenting. At this point, I'm in too deep. I can't just decide now that the kids aren't allowed in the bed. The younger ones will hold it against me.

> MY KID: Dad used to let the older kids sleep in the bed because he loves them way more.
>
> THERAPIST: That's okay. Your dad is burning in hell right now.
>
> MY KID: What a relief.

I don't want my kids to want me to burn in hell. I just want my bed back. Jeannie never seems to be bothered by the crowding. She would be comfortable under a blanket of children. Live children, of course.

Before it got crowded.

Morning Has Been Broken

I love sleep. I need sleep. We all do. Of course, there are those people that don't need sleep. I think they're called "success-ful." For me it's always a little sad getting out of bed. Every morning after I get up, I always gaze longingly at my bed and lament, "You were wonderful last night. I didn't want it to end. I can't wait to see you again . . ."

I am sure everyone reading this book values their sleep, but I am a sleep enthusiast! My dream is to become one of those grandpas in *Charlie and the Chocolate Factory* who just lives in bed. That looked awesome. There aren't many things that I let interfere with my sleep. Have you ever been asleep at night and you hear a noise you're convinced is a murderer that's trying to break into your house and kill you, but instead of getting up and escaping, you just go back to bed? I guess the reasoning is "They can't kill me if I'm asleep." I suppose that would be a pretty embarrassing way to die. That would create an awkward moment in heaven.

OTHER GUY IN HEAVEN: How did you die?

ME: I was too lazy to get out of bed. Yeah, I heard the guy in the kitchen. Thought I had an hour.

OTHER GUY IN HEAVEN: Wow. You're pretty lazy. How'd they let you in here?

ME: My wife got me in. She's over in the VIP section. Well, I should get back to cleaning up before I have to head back down to hell.

Sleep is too important. Sleep can make you give up any principle.

SOME GUY: Want to help the homeless?

ME: Sure. I'll help the homeless.

SOME GUY: Meet us Saturday morning at 7 a.m.

ME: [*Beat.*] Forget the homeless. They're homeless in the afternoon, too, right? Besides, I think they are big brunch people.

I used to have to negotiate with myself just to get out of bed. "All right, here's the deal, me. I'll get up, but I'm not taking a shower. I might be coming back here any minute." I used to hear the alarm in the morning "*Eee-eee-eee-eee*" and think, "I can get used to that. I'll just dream I'm in a techno club."

I gave up my relationship with sleep a long time ago. We had to break up even though neither of us wanted to. What came between us? Kids. Isn't that always the case? My kids were against me and sleep from the get-go. They gave me an ultimatum: us or sleep. Before I had time to make up my mind, sleep walked out on me and never came back. Someone should write a country song about it.

Sleep left me with full custody of my children. I'm usually awakened by a foot in my gut or my face, or a foot in my gut *and* a foot in my face. The result is I'm tired all the time. Even complaining how tired I am exhausts me. I'm so tired that the other day I tried to open my front door with my wallet.

Given how resistant children are to going to bed, I'm not surprised that they wake up so early. It's not just that they wake up early, it's *how* they wake up. I think *morning* means "speak louder" in little-kid language. My son does not address me in a whisper or even in a normal voice. He bellows three inches from my ear like we are four hundred feet apart. For some reason all my children speak the loudest in the morning. Of course, sometimes Jeannie will get up with the kids and "let me sleep," but the volume combined with the morning propensity toward temper tantrums makes this generous offer of "letting me sleep" an oxymoron. We have tried letting them stay up a little later so they sleep longer in the morning, but they just wake up more tired, more cranky, and, as a result, more LOUD.

The song goes, "Morning has broken," and I'm pretty sure my children broke it. Like everything else they break, if they did break it, they'll never admit it. I can just hear my kid's explanation.

SON: Morning was already broken, Dad.
ME: Really.
DAUGHTER: Yeah, we just came out here, and it was broken.

I don't know what's more exhausting about parenting: the getting up early or the acting like you know what you are doing. Sure, when I was single, I had to occasionally get up early for work, and it was a crisis!

"Jim, you have to get up next Tuesday at 7 a.m."

"Oh no! I should go to bed now!"

When you have kids, there is a whole different element of crisis. You are not only waking up sleep deprived, but now you are also sleep deprived and in charge of another human being. Not only are they absurdly loud in the morning, they are also ravenously hungry.

"Dad, I'm *starving*!"

"Go back to bed, it's too early."

"But I need to eat or I will *die*!"

Suddenly they turn into Oliver at the orphanage. Great, now if I don't get up, I am neglecting the basic needs of my child. Since Jeannie was against my brilliant idea of pouring cereal into dog bowls the night before, I have to get up and feed my kids.

TIME: 6 a.m.

SON: Daddy, we want pancakes!

ME ASLEEP: What? Who? You want what?

SON: Pancakes!

Great, he wants pancakes, and I feel like a pancake. It seems to me that if you are not old enough to make breakfast, you really should not be allowed to get up before 7 a.m. Of course, it doesn't feel like just getting up. It feels like punishment for every time in your life you complained about being bored. Now you are faced with the challenge of finding something in the house that they *want* to eat. They may be starving when they wake you up, but then they will complain about everything you try to give them.

Sometimes I'll make scrambled eggs for my kids, which usually barely get eaten. "They're too runny." "What is that, cheese? Ew." "Is there egg in this?" "I thought you were starving!" "I am, but not for *that!*" Unless it's an Easter basket or at IHOP, your little beggars become very choosy. Left to their own devices, they would probably just grab a bag of sugar and a spoon.

Once Marre, six at the time, made breakfast for herself and her brother and little sister. She woke us up and proudly announced, "You don't have to get up. I made breakfast for me, Jack, and Katie." When I asked why she had chocolate on her face, she explained they had breakfast dessert.

When I went out in the kitchen, it looked like a tornado had hit a frosting factory. Since Jeannie is usually breastfeeding a baby at this time of the morning, I normally get blamed for these natural disasters.

JEANNIE: What happened out here?
ME: The kids made breakfast dessert.
JEANNIE: Have fun cleaning it up.

Most mornings it feels like it takes more than a village.

Naps Are Payday Loans

Given my passion for sleep, it is no surprise how I feel about naps. I believe in naps. I like to think of naps as a nonverbal way of saying to life, "I quit. I'm sitting this part of the day out." I understand that naps are usually reserved for babies and old people, but I don't discriminate. Naps used to be an integral part of my everyday life. Prior to children, a catastrophe for me was when I would sleep so late in the morning that I would miss my nap.

As a new parent, I was pleased to discover that newborns take a lot of naps. It seems like they nap more than they are awake. Newborns nap so much, you'd think they were on drugs or depressed. Always looking to contribute, I'll often selflessly offer to help get one of our babies to sleep. Sometimes I'll nap with our fifteen-month-old son to be supportive. Sometimes I'll nap with our newborn to be supportive. Sometimes I'll nap alone in homage to our newborn and fifteen-month-old. It's all about putting kids first, really.

Any parent can tell you how important it is for children up to age two to take a nap. With babies, you always want to avoid the dreaded "over tired" state, and nobody wants to be around a two-year-old who didn't nap. You'll never hear a parent say, "He didn't nap today" about a two-year-old boy that is behaving well. Naps are a necessity.

Unfortunately, around the age of three, there comes a time when napping your child becomes counterproductive. It's not worth it. The nap during the day for a three-year-old becomes a payday loan. For those of you who don't understand the connection, a payday loan is for people who can't seem to make ends meet until their next paycheck, so they go to a loan company (aka thieves) that will give them their paycheck amount early for a huge fee. This is of course unwise, and Suze Orman would be angry with you.

It is equally unwise when applied to napping. If you take the payday loan of some free time by letting your cranky, drowsy three-year-old succumb to the relinquished nap habit, be prepared that your child will be awake very late. When I say awake, I really mean a nuisance to your life and sanity. This is the aforementioned huge fee that you now must pay.

When I say late, I mean late. A three-year-old with insomnia is very similar to a heroin addict going through withdrawal. There is nothing that calms them. They can't focus. You can't tell them enough stories. They don't understand why they are still awake four hours past their bedtime. This is commonly understood by all parents of three-year-olds and has inspired great works of literature, such as *Go the F-ck to Sleep.*

Sure, while your three-year-old naps during the day, you

can get some work done, nap yourself, or waste time on the Internet, but at what cost? Now it's payday, and you squandered your loan on what? Checking Twitter? Somebody call Suze, because you need advice.

Once you have figured out the horrible consequences of the payday loan, you become obsessed with preventing the nap-weaned three-year-old from napping in the middle of the day at all costs. This is not easy. They have napped all their life. They want to nap. They need to nap. You would like them a lot better if they napped. You feel that by keeping them awake, you are putting them through some CIA sleep-deprivation experiment. It seems cruel, yet you find yourself dreaming up ways to keep them awake: "You're nodding off at four p.m? Time for a cold bath and a hot cup of coffee!"

Then comes the impossible task of enforcing nap prevention when your child is in the care of others. It's understandable that babysitters love napping children. "She was a delight!" is always code for "She slept for four hours!" Jeannie and I have strict orders to not let Katie fall asleep, but why should the babysitters comply? They will never encounter the consequences of napping a three-year-old. Now we are the naive co-signers that wind up footing the bill when the sitter defaults. The housing crisis could have easily been prevented if someone had simply explained the economics of napping a three-year-old. Prepare for foreclosure on your evening because there's no bailout in sight.

Get Married, Have Kids, Get Fat

I'm getting fat . . . as I planned. Luckily, my gut is intentional. I'm actually preparing for a big role. Sure, it's a cinnamon roll, but I want there to be room for it. Okay, fine, I could lose some weight, but I'm not going to hide behind some lame excuse. My paunch is no one's fault but my kids'.

I'm gaining weight, and I do blame my kids. I suppose that's the cliché, right? You get married, you have kids, and you get fat. It's not like being around young children suddenly makes you hungry. It's just being around what children *eat*. Have you seen what a six-year-old wants to eat? "I'll have a slice of pizza, a chocolate milk, and a lollipop." Like they are on some drug-induced munchie binge. "For dinner, get me mac and cheese, a handful of pretzels, and half of a cupcake."

They don't actually ask for half of a cupcake, but half a cupcake is all they'll actually eat. Once my daughter Katie ate the icing off a cupcake and then asked for more cake on her bread.

Half-eaten is an important detail. What are you supposed to do with the other half of that cupcake? A three-year-old will never finish their food. I'll take my kids out to dinner, and they'll leave half a plate of french fries. What? Who would actually *leave* french fries? It's not some self-control thing. They aren't thinking, "Moment on the lips, forever on the hips." They just get distracted. "What's that shiny thing over there?" Now I'm supposed to eat a boring-ass healthy salad when there's a half a plate of fries twelve inches from me just going to waste? This is why being a parent is like the opposite of the Jenny Craig diet. I can just see the pitch: "I gained twenty pounds just eating small portions of my children's leftovers. And it works!"

Now some of you might be thinking, why don't I just order something healthy for my kids? Well, that's not possible in a restaurant. Have you ever noticed that the children's menu is exactly the same as the bar menu? Burger, hot dog, pizza. If you put the children's menu at the bar, people wouldn't even notice. "Oh, cool. I can color in an airplane while I drink this beer and wait for my chicken strips."

Of course, there is a reason why there is no outrage that the children's menu is the same as the bar menu. At a restaurant, the "I want my kids to eat healthy" rules are literally off the table. As a society, we are all concerned about childhood obesity until we bring a kid into a restaurant and want that kid to be quiet. Then even the most health-conscious mom changes her tune. "Yes, you can have cake and ice cream. Now what do you want for dessert?" Being at a restaurant with small children is not the time or place to enforce the "eat all your broccoli first" rule unless you want everyone in the restaurant to hate you. "Your children are so well behaved!" No they're not—they're sedated with deep-fried chicken strips.

Obviously, what a child eats at home is entirely the parent's responsibility. Kids will eat other things besides fries and hot dogs. I should be clear that Jeannie only buys "organic" food, which I believe is a grocery term for "twice as expensive." I've almost gotten used to eating a type of "sprouted" bread that I believe is made from tree bark. Thanks to Jeannie's leadership, instead of eating junk food, our kids eat organic junk food. You make as many smart choices as you can, but the war of attrition eventually involves you relenting to the whining. "Fine, here's an organic pizza roll."

It's always been hard for me to eat healthy, but with kids, it's virtually impossible. To people without young kids, allow me to explain. A kid doesn't have to be spoiled or exposed to bad habits; it can happen in an instant. You would never buy desserts to have around the house if you want your kids to eat healthy, but you might innocently have cake after dinner one night. A special treat, right? What you don't realize is that to a five-year-old, you have now established a precedent. One piece of cake on one night has ushered in six weeks of "What's for dessert?" You might say, "It's Tuesday. There is no dessert." Now, to a five-year-old, that only means *try harder for dessert.* "But a month and a half ago, we had cake after dinner. That's how we do it now." It doesn't matter that it was their birthday. Now they expect it, and if they don't get it, they give you this look like they are being deprived. So then you have the brilliant idea to start using it as a punishment: If you don't do this, then no dessert! Which means now you have put yourself in a position where you are forced to actually have some dessert around in the event of the slim chance they actually do behave. So you must forsake your convictions and start buying desserts. This predicament is called "being stranded on a dessert island."

Hand-in-Mouth Disease

Overall, kids are horrible at eating. We all know a baby's first food experience is always a disaster. Anyone who has ever fed a baby his first cereal or strained carrots knows that calling this experience "eating" is generous. It is really a ritual that simply entails smearing a baby with food. The chance that some may actually end up in his mouth is purely incidental.

The next step in the evolution of eating is when a baby is learning to pick up food and "feed" himself. Watching a nine-month-old try to find his mouth is a game of pin the tail on the donkey. The food ends up in his ears, eyes, nose, and hair, but, again, rarely the mouth.

You would think a couple of years of practice would be enough for these babies to figure how to eat. After all, you can get an MBA degree in the same amount of time. Unfortunately, eating with children aged two to six years old is not that much of an improvement. First off, getting them to sit in a chair at the table is an accomplishment. Once they are there, getting them to properly use utensils is a feat. I don't have to explain how fast kids can turn a simple butter knife into a shiv. A full spoon will be empty by the time it reaches the mouth. Little kids may start off with a fork, but eventually they'll return to their trusty hands, because inevitably that fork is on the floor within five seconds of the kid picking it up. Eating with their hands seems to be the preferred method by a long shot.

Most of the time, I feel like I'm eating with a tribe of Bedouins . . . except for the fact that Bedouins actually eat *over* their plates. Kids don't bother to eat over their plates. It normally appears as if they are attempting to NOT eat over their plates. This is why there is no difference between a four-year-old eating a taco and throwing a taco on the floor. The amount of food on the floor under the table where a kid is eating could be the solution to world hunger. And if there is ever a fork shortage, they could solve that crisis under that same table. The beverages, however, are normally knocked over *on* the table, where they can wreak the most havoc.

A little kid spilling a drink at the dinner table is as reliable as the female lead falling down in a romantic comedy. It's inevitable. The moment you forget about it or think it won't happen, it happens. To be fair, one time our two-year-old went for an entire dinner without spilling her drink. She spilled mine instead. Most of the time, you watch the spill happen, and you are powerless to stop it. Time always seems to move in slow motion as you sit paralyzed, watching the tiny hand or elbow clumsily knocking into the side of a cup. It feels like hours after you've cried "Noooo!" before the glass actually tips over, soaking everything in sight. The only surprising aspect of the spilled drink is the consistency of the little kid's reaction to it: There *is* no reaction. They do nothing. They don't attempt to clean it up with a napkin or curb the extent of the damage by picking up the cup. Nothing. They just watch the spill, fascinated as it splits into steams, channels, and tributaries, as if they are hoping for a salmon to jump out. As a parent, you react in the exact opposite way. You overreact. As if your yelp is somehow going to help stop this inevitable event. It's your *Groundhog Day* moment. The spill happens every day, but unlike Bill Murray, you somehow don't get more adept at dealing with the consequences. This is of course why God invented sippy cups.

For parents, sippy cups are to the beverage what pizza is to the food. If there was a flag for parents of small children, it would have a sippy cup and a slice of pizza on it. By the way, the sippy cup would have nonmatching parts, and the pizza would be only partially eaten if anyone wants to be the Betsy Ross of the kiddie food flag.

It's easy to understand why pizza is the official food of early childhood. Kids love pizza. Pizza makes kids way happier than the Happy Meal, and it doesn't even have to come with a toy.

If you meet a kid who doesn't like pizza in some form, I recommend counseling. Pizza is fun. Pizza is a synonym for *party*. Here are my instructions on how to throw a really great pizza party. Step one: Order pizza. That's it.

Pizza is the answer to kids' eating problems I mentioned earlier. Pizza is so easy. Kids don't need utensils to eat a pizza. Hell, you don't even need a plate. The crust is the built-in edible plate. Pizza makes you a hero in the eyes of your kids. "Daddy got pizza!" You are higher status walking in the door with a pizza than if you were returning from a war with a Purple Heart. Pizza is easy to order and easy to clean up, but here's the rub: pizza is horrible for you. As an adult, even the unhealthiest of us understand that we should eat pizza roughly once a year or we'll look like someone who, well, looks like they eat pizza all the time.

Unfortunately, if you have young kids you *will* eat pizza all the time. Well, it will feel like all the time. If kids are celebrating *anything*, there will be pizza. For the last couple of years, Friday night has been "pizza night" in our home, and I've grown to dread it. I never get a chance to crave or even want pizza anymore.

It's sad for me to see the shift in my attitude toward pizza. I've loved it all my life. It was a treat in my childhood, a staple in college, and a terrific late-night snack after shows, but now that's all gone. Pizza has become that old buddy who was really fun to hang out with, but now he shows up at your house all the time uninvited, trying to make you fat, and you are like, "Dude, I know we used to party together, but you really need to get a life." Like sleep and silence, my love for pizza has become another casualty of parenting.

We Need Bread

I like taking my kids to eat at places like diners, IHOP, and Waffle House. They eat like five dollars' worth of food and do like forty dollars' worth of damage to the restaurant. I don't even feel guilty. You won't exactly find these places in a Michelin Guide.

Every six months or so, I make the disastrous error of taking my five children out to dinner at a nice restaurant. Now, "nice restaurant" can have many meanings, so let's just say a restaurant that has cloth napkins that no normal human would bring five little kids into. I don't know how or why I could ever forget what a mistake it is taking an eight-year-old, a six-year-old, a three-year-old, a one-year-old, and a newborn into a nice restaurant, but I always do. As we are walking to our table, it is clear that everyone eating in the restaurant knows that it's a gigantic mistake. The waiter always knows. The entire restaurant staff has the same look on their face, like, "Are you sure you want to do this?"

What little kids bring to the table is the direct opposite of everything people enjoy about having dinner in a nice restaurant; sitting, waiting patiently, enjoying the ambience, not being around obnoxiousness. Sure, sometimes a three-year-old will sit quietly and not lick the top of a salt shaker, but an experienced parent knows they are just ticking time bombs. Three-year-olds only sit down for two reasons. And let's just say the other one is eating. Just eating. Not having a conversation and then eating. Not hearing about the specials and then eating. Not enjoying the atmosphere and then eating. Just eating, and soon after that, the other reason that three-year-olds sit down.

It is for this reason that any parent of young children knows you must feed them immediately, if not sooner, in a restaurant. If there is not bread on the table a minicrisis ensues. I truly feel for any waiter or waitress that gets our table.

> **WAITER:** Hi, I'm Todd. Would you guys like to hear about our spec—
> **ME:** Can we please have bread? We need bread, or these kids will tear this place apart. If you don't have bread, just bring out a chew toy or a bone to occupy them. Trust me. I'm looking out for everyone in this restaurant.

A conscientious waiter will respond as if I've told him we have to evacuate and he won't have time to gather his possessions. The kids will get bread, their drink, and their food, and then Jeannie, myself, and all of the other diners will enjoy their food in peace. Instead of this, we normally get the waiter who seems to have never had any interaction with young children. We are always educating them: "Please bring the kids' meals as soon as they are ready." A lot of waiters at fancy restaurants are really way too occupied with the proper order of service: drinks, appetizers, soup, salad, entrée, dessert, coffee. Their training and the rules supersede our knowledge of what will happen if the kids have to wait for food. When we are with our kids, we don't care the slightest bit about the etiquette of fine dining. Just bring the kids their food first. Despite our clear request, on many occasions Jeannie and I have actually gotten our meals first. In what universe would we be able to eat our dinners when our kids have nothing in front of them except glass and steel weapons?

Half the battle is to keep the kids seated at the table and for me to not drive a steak knife in my throat for being so dumb as to bring a three-year-old to a nice restaurant. By design, nicer restaurants don't have crayons to occupy the children. Often we have to improvise. "Here, play with my phone." "Here's some gum." "Enjoy this pack of matches." It's amazing how many ways you can fold a cocktail napkin to creatively transform it into something unique like a smaller folded cocktail napkin.

Really nice restaurants don't have a children's menu option. In this case, I always suggest ordering plain pasta with olive oil. Anything else you order will be an enormous waste of money and time. The fancier the entrée, the less likely your kid will want to eat it.

Every Thanksgiving I do shows in Las Vegas at The Mirage, and the whole gang comes. Last year we went to a fine-dining restaurant for the Thanksgiving meal. When we heard that they had a special of soup that was festively served in miniature pumpkins, we ignorantly thought the kids would be delighted. Below is my then seven-year-old daughter's critique of the amazing fifteen-dollar pumpkin soup she didn't even try.

Aside from the plain pasta, I have another brilliant piece of wisdom for those of you who want to enjoy yourselves while eating at a fine restaurant with your small children: Don't bring them. You're welcome.

You Win, McDonald's

It's just too easy. I'm sorry. I know McDonald's is horrible for you, and taking my children to McDonald's is irresponsible. I even understand the evil behind the "Happy Meal." A free toy with a meal? It's evil genius. Just like a divorced parent, McDonald's knows if you want a child to come back, you have to bribe them. I know McDonald's is essentially buying another generation of consumers. Even crack dealers find McDonald's unscrupulous. But McDonald's is too easy. They could provide small packs of cigarettes in every Happy Meal and I still would go to McDonald's on long car rides with my children.

> **ME:** Okay, honey, you can have the apple dippers with the jug of caramel dipping sauce, but not the cigarettes.
> **FIVE-YEAR-OLD:** Just one?
> **ME:** All right, just one. But don't smoke when you're pregnant.

Anyone who has had to travel over an hour with a little kid in a car has been to McDonald's. All experienced parents eventually reach the same conclusion. "Why should I stop at McDonald's and get my kid crappy chicken nuggets when I could wait until we get to the hotel and get my kids crappy chicken strips for twenty dollars?" McDonald's wins. You don't have to get out of your car. You are taking your kids out to dinner, but you don't have to take them out to dinner. You don't have to clean any dishes. The box that the Happy Meal comes in transforms magically into a mini garbage can. You even already know how disappointed you are going to feel about going there. You win, McDonald's.

It's not just traveling. McDonald's is an amazing bargaining chip with your children. "If you keep behaving like that, I'm not taking you to McDonald's." I mentioned earlier that my father would force me and my siblings to do yard work every Saturday for hours when I was growing up. What I failed to mention is that my father would reward us by taking us to McDonald's at the end of the day. It seemed like a great deal when I was eight. Of course, the irony is that my dad had to feed us anyway. "[*Cough.*] How about you do eight hours of yard work and in exchange I'll feed you dinner?" Deal. Of course, we would have been fed dinner, but this was McDonald's.

Really, the best and worst part about taking your kids to McDonald's is that you find yourself at McDonald's. The strongest willpower melts away. You have an excuse, a justification, for eating McDonald's. "Well, I'm here anyway. Guess I have to get the Quarter Pounder with Cheese."

I've even mastered justifying a stop at a McDonald's drive-thru when all my kids are asleep. "Hey! We finally found a McDonald's! Oh, the kids are asleep. Well, I'm here anyway. Guess I have to get the Quarter Pounder with Cheese." You win, McDonald's.

How Sweet It Is

I'm assuming everyone reading this was a kid at one time. Well, most of you were. I don't have to tell you how important candy is to children. Candy is the currency of children. Kids collect it, trade it, and hoard it. It's how parents bribe their kids. It's how annoying kids get friends. I'm sure I wasn't the only kid thinking, "I don't really like that neighbor boy, but he always has candy, so it looks like we are going to hang out a lot." As a kid, it was baffling to contemplate the adult blasé attitude toward candy. I remember thinking, "When I'm an adult and have a job, I'm going to spend all my money on candy." Of course, as you get older, your taste buds change, you start getting acne, and eventually you decide you don't want to be a fat tub of turds. You realize that you have to set boundaries with candy. By that I mean you decide to never buy candy or willfully be around it.

As an adult, I always wondered who was buying the candy

that seemed to be sold everywhere. I never understood why they even had candy on display in front of the cash register at drugstores. Who is that for? "Yeah, while you're ringing up my diabetes medication, throw in this Snickers." They put that candy right at a child's eye level so the parent will be fumbling with their wallet at checkout and their kids beg them for the candy and they give in out of frustration. Not me. I am not falling for that evil marketing scheme like those other suckers. I would never purchase candy, and obviously I would never give candy to my children.

Yet for some reason, now that I have kids, I eat candy all the time. I've never *bought* the candy, but it is constantly ending up in my house—it's my children's candy that we have confiscated for safekeeping. Suddenly I have this big bowl of temptation in my cupboard beckoning me to eat it. It doesn't have to be good candy. I've eaten an entire bag of stale gummy bears on more than one occasion—in the past month.

I don't think of it as stealing. Hey, it's my home, and those kids don't pay rent. Most of the time I don't even *want* to eat their candy, but late at night I'm confronted with the predicament: eat my kids' candy or feel my feelings. Eating the candy always seems to win. Now, there are parents who would not raid their children's stash, and they are called weirdos or anorexic. What would *you* do if you had a bag of mini chocolate bars in your house? Let your kids eat it? Throw it away? I'm pretty sure throwing away candy is a crime in some states. Let's be serious, you would eat the candy. You would eat the candy to save your children's lives. It's a heroic action, actually. (By the way, I'm not eating *all* of my children's candy. When I pilfer their Halloween bags every year, I take only the Snickers, Reese's, and Heath Bars. I thoughtfully leave them the Now and Laters, Wax Lips, and the wrappers. I'm not a criminal.)

Future generations will look back on our propensity to give candy to children as something preposterous, like giving cigarettes to babies. Sometimes it feels like candy is being forced on parents. My son's preschool had an annual fundraiser that involved selling a case of chocolate bars. Really? Chocolate bars? Part of why we are sending our kids to preschool is so they wouldn't be at home begging for candy. This always felt comparable to raising money to fight heart disease by selling steaks. A three-year-old is not going to go around selling chocolate bars. I certainly am not going to go around selling chocolate bars. The solution? Write a check, and Dad eats a case of chocolate bars.

Don't worry, my kids barely notice any of their candy is gone. Recently my eight-year-old, Marre, asked, "What happened to my Valentine's Day candy?" Like a good parent, I lied: "I don't know." Not missing a beat, she responded, "Oh well, I'll just have some of my Easter candy."

There's always another birthday party, another holiday. Birthdays and holidays are just drug mules smuggling candy to our children, and we are the corrupt DEA agents fighting the losing war on candy.

For today's kids, it's an abundant candy universe. They don't even have to try for it; they are of the "treat bag" generation. Sure, my children still beg us for it, but that is because they know we have it. When I was a kid, we never had candy in our house. It was a reserved fantasy that came true on Halloween.

You would binge on it one night a year after trick-or-treating, have a horrible stomachache the next day, and spend the rest of the year dreaming about candy. I remember watching a Rolo commercial as a kid and longingly thinking, "One day . . ."

Before I wrap this essay up and eat some of my kids' candy, I do need to address two candies in particular. One is evil, and one is a lifesaver, and no, I'm not talking about Life Savers.

Gum

Probably the most destructive candy is chewing gum. Ever give a three-year-old a piece of gum? It always seems like a good idea: it will keep them occupied; it's not candy, so they won't be ingesting handfuls of it, and all little kids absolutely love gum. If they know you have a pack of gum, you suddenly have absolute power. You can lord it over them: "If you behave in the supermarket, I will give you a piece of gum." Kids will do anything for a piece of gum.

Of course, you think that the worst thing that can happen is that they will swallow the gum. "Don't swallow the gum! It takes seven years to digest!" In reality, you should encourage them to swallow the gum, because the worst thing that can happen is them losing the gum. A lost piece of chewed gum will wreak havoc on everything in sight and end up in places that will shock you. Kids cannot keep gum in their mouth. Half the fun of gum to a three-year-old is stretching it out, rolling it in a ball like chewable Play-Doh, and eventually losing it somewhere. You will discover that that piece of gum somehow has fused itself to the butt of your pants and become intermingled with the fabric of your jeans forever. Give a kid gum, and the bad karma is instantaneous. That gum is guaranteed to somehow find its way into the clothes dryer and ruin all the school uniforms at once.

The other day I submitted to the begging of my three-year-old, Katie, and gave her a piece of gum that five seconds later was firmly embedded in her hair. She had to get that emergency haircut with that isolated spike that screams, "I was playing with scissors," or "My idiot dad gave me gum." I don't want to get all political, but I am definitely pro–gum control.

Lollipops

My kids love lollipops, but not as much as I love lollipops. My love of lollipops is not about eating them; it's about how quiet they make my children. It is virtually impossible for a three-year-old to whine and complain with a lollipop in her mouth. "Waaah! I don't want to sit in the ba—[*suck, suck*]. This one is cherry."

If you ever take your kids to a situation where they must be quiet, bring lollipops. They're like flavored muzzles. Mothers-to-be should be given bouquets of lollipops at baby showers. At the hospital, people should hand lollipops to new fathers and say, "Here, you're going to need this." It's the parent's secret weapon. What about the sugar? Well, Dr. John makes sugar-free lollipops. (No, he did not pay me to write that. He does not even know who I am. I don't even know if Dr. John is a real doctor or if he even exists. I have to assume lollipop Dr. John is different from the musician Dr. John, who sang that song "Right Place, Wrong Time." By coincidence, that song could be used to describe any parent with a kid who needs a lollipop. Dr. John is most likely not the musician and just the "Mama Celeste" of lollipops. Of course, if you do exist, Dr. John, I think you should send me a case of sugar-free lollipops as a reward for mentioning you.)

A rare moment of silence from Katie and Jack.

There is no sugar in Dr. John's lollipops. They are sweetened with a natural sweetener that we will likely find out in ten years is a hundred times worse for you than sugar. The sugar predicament is strange. It's always like, "Sugar's bad! Sugar will rot your teeth and make you fat! Use these yellow packets instead." Then, like six months later: "Don't use those yellow packets—they cause cancer! They even cause worse cancer than those pink packets of fake sugar we told you caused cancer six months ago." You are always forced to face the dilemma "Do I eat the sugar that will make me fat, *or* do I use this other stuff that will kill me? Hmmm. Eh, what's a little cancer? Cancer makes you lose weight, right?" What was I talking about? Oh, yes. Lollipops. Why did you change the subject and start talking about that other thing that no one wants to say out loud? After all, this is a book about kids and being a good-looking dad.

'Tis the Season

Kids love holidays. As a kid, I used to measure the year by which holiday was coming up. The most important time of the year was the "Holiday Season"—the period between Thanksgiving and New Year's Day. It encompassed so many holidays, including Hanukkah, Christmas, that African one that's even harder to spell than Hanukkah, and many others. That time period is clearly a season of holidays. A holiday season. No matter what faith you belong to or what tradition you follow, everyone is partying. You're shopping, you're cooking, you're getting together with family, you're eating food that's bad for you, you're eating more food that's bad for you, and of course you're eating food that's bad for you.

Holidays are also an opportunity for kids to unlearn every good habit they've learned during the rest of the year. They don't go to school. They get to stay up past their bedtime. They get candy and presents for doing nothing. Childhood utopia.

The "Holiday Season" was always the longest one, so it was obviously my favorite.

Now what's happened since I was a kid is that all holidays have become "holiday seasons." If you don't believe me, go into any drugstore. The day after New Year's Day, the Valentine's Day aisle appears. The day after Valentine's Day, the same aisle is filed with shamrocks and leprechauns.

Halloween is no longer one night. It's a week if you're lucky. A month if you live in New York City. I don't know how this happened or what the logic was. "Well, Halloween lands on a Tuesday, so let's have the kids dress up every day for a month." There are even Halloween greeting cards now. As a result of this extended Halloween "season," kids end up having more than one Halloween costume, like they are competing in a beauty pageant. "What costume do you want to wear to school?" Then "What costume do you want to wear to the parade?" Then "What costume do you want to wear to trick-or-treat?" Then "What costume do you want to wear to the swimsuit competition?" When I was growing up, I barely had a Halloween costume. I mostly remember cutting a couple of holes in a sheet for eyes and going as a ghost. Wait, maybe that was just in that Charlie Brown's Halloween special. I just remember going as either a ghost or a bum. Not a homeless person, but a bum. It was a less sensitive era.

Now there is mandatory parental participation in holidays when you have young children. Of course you want to share the experience with them, but no matter how jaded you might be, you just dare not ruin it for them. The tradition of chopping down a pine tree and putting it in your living room may seem like the behavior of a drunk guy, but you do it sober. You carve pumpkins, paint eggs, anything for your kids. Somehow a couple of years ago, I even became one of those dads who dresses up with his kids at Halloween.

This is how much I love my kids.

I can't believe it either. Yes, it was Jeannie's idea, and I've done it more than once. I just wish I had known before how similar Captain Hook looks to Captain Morgan when you run into drunk people who really like rum on Halloween.

Even though my kids still measure the year by holidays, there is barely any downtime between them. Add in birthday parties, and the fun never stops. If the holidays used to be a time that kids unlearned their good habits, now the five minutes between holidays are the only time for them to unlearn their bad habits. This holiday conspiracy created by the evil drugstore corporate giants is threatening to create an entire generation of spoiled monsters. Just another hurdle for parents who don't want a house full of these holiday-possessed demons but also don't want to be the only parents who threaten to "cancel Christmas" every time their kids misbehave. You become caught on the horns of a dilemma. When your treat-bag-generation kids are getting treats constantly, you lose the specialness of treating them yourselves. Now, truly the only way to really treat your kids as a reward for good behavior is to *not* treat them to treats. And then you know you are treating them well. I think my head just exploded.

This is how bad I need a drink.

My Other Family

Holidays inevitably mean family gatherings. For parents of young children, these become mandatory. No matter how you feel about your extended family or family gatherings you will be attending. This is because now the ultimate reason for attending family gatherings is for your children to have the time of their lives with their cousins.

Little kids *love* their cousins. I'm not being cute or exaggerating here. Cousins are like celebrities for little kids. If little kids had a *People* magazine, cousins would be on the cover. Cousins are the barometers of how fun a family get-together will be. "Are the cousins going to be there? Fun!" Of course, the reason cousins seem so special could be because they are always associated with positive events. Holidays, birthdays, summer vacations. Cousins are always at the right parties. There are always presents, candy, and swimming time with cousins. That is the cousin conundrum. Cousins are like cake. Does the cake make the event fun, or is it the fun event that makes you like cake? Personally, I think it's the cake. Doesn't the word *cake* make you want cake? Ah, cake. What was I talking about?

Most of my kids haven't even figured out that the parents of their precious cousins are actually children of siblings of Jeannie or me. "Wait, you're Uncle Joe's brother? What a coincidence!" To a child, there's this intangible quality in a cousin. They are like brothers and sisters, but you don't see them enough to get sick of them. The children of your siblings are God's trick to keep you coming to family gatherings. "My extended family makes me crazy . . . , but the kids love it."

I don't want you to think I don't love my extended family. I do. I just don't want to be around them. Some of this is because I'm a loner. Some of this is because at family gatherings you are forced to face the short genetic distance between you and a clinically insane person. As a result, family gatherings always seem to coincide with brief periods of alcohol abuse on my part. I don't drink that often, but when I get around my family— Glug, glug, glug. We're not even arguing. "Good to see you." Glug, glug, glug. "Yeah we had another kid." Glug, glug, glug. It's not just me. Everyone is drinking. Everything is an excuse to drink in my family. "Hey, it's Fourth of July, have a beer." "Hey, I haven't seen you in a while, have a beer." "Hey, you're throwing up, have a beer." I've never seen my family tree, and I think this is because someone chopped it down and built a bar with it.

Family gatherings are strange. Honestly, I'm always excited for family gatherings. "This is going to be great!" Then roughly a half hour later, I'm on the phone.

"How much would it cost to change my ticket?

"To this afternoon.

"Well, I'm at the airport now.

"Can I wait on the runway?

"I need to get out of here now!"

Of course, there's a built-in forgetter with family. You only remember when you get there. "Oh, that's right. Everyone's crazy! No wonder I live three thousand miles away." Glug, glug, glug. Mankind has made amazing advancements over the centuries, but we can't remember our family is crazy. I bet cavemen remembered. "Me know every day yellow ball go down from sky, and my extended family is bonkers." That is why the holidays are spaced out like they are. The day after the Fourth of July, you always tell yourself, "I'm never dealing with those weirdos again." The day before Thanksgiving, "It's going to be great to see everyone again." Glug, glug, glug.

Are You Done Yet?

I have five children, and I don't even own a farm. Traditionally, big families were necessary to help with the harvest, and there was also an understanding that some children may be lost to disease. Alas, it is a different era than *Little House on the Prairie*. Now we have tractors, and everyone is going to make it through the winter. Big families are very rare today. When I was growing up, it wasn't uncommon to have a friend who came from a big family. As a matter of fact, we lived down the street from a family that had thirteen children. That seemed like a big family. Today, big families are like waterbed stores; they used to be everywhere, and now they are just weird. Admit it, whenever you see a waterbed store, you think, "Wow. That has to be a front for something illegal." Big families are even more rare in New York City, where we live. When strangers find out I have five children, it usually makes even the toughest, most jaded New Yorker concerned. "Five kids? Are you creating your own nationality?"

Based on some reactions to hearing that I have five children, it seems as though people think that I'm ignorant of the fact that having five children is a huge task. People will say instructively, "Five kids, that's a lot." As if they're educating me. Oh, really? I thought it was a small number of children. Wait, is "one" a smaller number than "five" or a larger number? I always get those two confused. Can I borrow your calculator?

Many times people say, "I don't know how you handle five kids. I have one kid, and I can barely handle it!" Well, guess what? One kid is a lot. I could barely handle having one kid. I guess it's kind of like that science experiment with the frog in a pot where you slowly turn the heat up on the water, degree by degree, so the frog doesn't figure out what's happening until he's boiling and it's too late. Well, I am that frog. I didn't suddenly become the father of five children. That would be really overwhelming. Not that I'm *not* overwhelmed. At this point, the feeling of being overwhelmed overwhelms me. Thankfully, the pregnancies and babies came one by one, each with their unique hurdles and victories. But the most entertaining gauge of our growing family was the mounting scale of reactions from friends and family.

We found out Jeannie was pregnant with Marre five weeks after we returned from our honeymoon. Yes, Jeannie is that fertile, or I'm that good at making babies. Or both. The point is, everyone was thrilled. There was a baby shower. There was endless advice from friends who already had a kid. "Say good-bye to your sex life." (This always seems like a strange thing to say to anyone at any time.) Well, we didn't say good-bye to it at all. In fact, ten months later, Jeannie got pregnant with our first son, Jack. Again, everyone was thrilled. There wasn't a baby shower this time, but there was more advice from friends with two kids on how to deal. "You are *really* in for it now!" After two kids, a boy and a girl, you start hearing things like, "Well, now you've got one of each! Perfect!" To me the message was clear: "You guys should stop."

When we found out we were having our third child, Katie, I felt we started losing the crowd. The congratulations were always preceded by a *wow*. "Wow . . . congratulations!" The one couple we knew with three kids gave us advice about dealing with three little ones. "Now you're outnumbered!" Then came the fourth pregnancy, Michael, and everything changed. There was audible nervousness in our friends' and families' congratulations, which included multiple *wows*. "Wow . . . congratulations . . . wow, wow!" In certain parts of the country, having four kids is not strange at all. In New York City, it is equivalent to having a thousand. I felt like friends started treating us like we were Amish and voluntarily living without electricity.

"Well, that's one way to live your life. Hey, can you build me one of those wood fireplaces?" We were treated like pioneers. The couple we knew with three kids showed us a map of Utah. We were questioned as if we were curious oddities at a freak show. "What's that like?" I explained what it was like having a fourth kid very simply: imagine you are drowning . . . and then someone hands you a baby.

In a strange way, four kids made us celebrities. At school pickups, I was no longer introduced as a comedian, I was "the father of four." Strangely, there was some sympathy, too, as if something horrible just "happened" to me, like a tornado blowing the roof off of my house. I remember an unemployed father telling me to "hang in there." Everyone knows that when someone shows you sympathy, you do the natural thing. You play into it for your own benefit. I started using the four kids as an excuse for everything. "Sorry I'm late . . . I have four kids." "I know I've put on some weight, but I do have four kids." "Sorry, I have four kids, I have four kids."

While these births and subsequent reactions of friends and family were happening, we were living in a two-bedroom apartment roughly the size of an airplane bathroom. This was another source of entertainment for the peanut gallery. "Well, at least you thought it through." We were constantly searching for another apartment in Manhattan that we could afford—and not just squeeze into for another year before we would have to start looking again. We were juggling schedules with kids at three different schools in three different parts of town. Jeannie was producing my third one-hour comedy special while nursing our eight-month-old Michael when we got a big positive on a pregnancy test. If having four kids is drowning and someone hands you a baby, then the fifth kid is the same scenario but with a shark fin coming at you. How would I tell my friends and family that we just found out we were expecting a fifth? We had left the realm of normalcy. After Jeannie and I went to the scary ultrasound place (always a relaxing experience) and saw our fifth child, Patrick, I decided to just announce it on Twitter. I didn't even want to process the *wows* of friends and family in person. I knew that to them we had become that disappointing friend on yet another trip to rehab. They weren't even rooting for us anymore. We were the soldier volunteering for his fifth tour of Afghanistan. We were on our own. In their eyes, we had "jumped the shark." All of a sudden, four kids seemed a lot more normal. We immediately started getting compared to people with absurd numbers of children. "My great-great-aunt had sixteen kids." Well, tell her I said hi. "Are you trying to catch up with the Duggars?" Yes, we are. We only need fourteen more children and we will win!

When Jeannie and I brought our fifth child, Patrick, to his first doctor's visit, we waited for an elevator with a mother and her three young kids. The mother proudly corralled the energetic ten-, seven-, and five-year-olds onto the elevator. When her five-year-old asked if Jeannie's sling was holding a baby, the mother warned her kids to be careful and not to touch the newborn. Jeannie pulled down the side of the sling to reveal one-day-old Patrick. The nice kids swooned at seeing the tiny baby. The mother confidently asked, "Is this your first?" When Jeannie replied that it was our fifth, the mother's demeanor changed. "Are you kidding me? Five? Really? FIVE?" Then came the most popular reaction. The question that has become an integral part of our daily life: "Are you guys *done* yet?"

When Jeannie gave birth to Patrick, I was not surprised by the absence of congratulatory calls, flowers, and baby gifts. These steadily dropped off after the second child. We certainly didn't need any more baby clothes at that point. Heck, after Jeannie gave birth to our fourth, Michael, I barely received an e-mail acknowledgment from most of my siblings. I get it. "Another baby from Jim and Jeannie." It held the ceremony of renewing an annual health club membership. I understand. However, I *was* surprised how often so many people asked, "Are you guys done yet?" I'm always tempted to reply, "Why do you ask? Are you paying their college tuition?" I feel as if I'm under so much pressure to make the decision at that moment. "Are you done yet?" Like we are the last patrons in a restaurant at midnight, lingering over dessert, and the waiter has a train to catch. "Are you done yet? Anything else? Can I get those plates out of your way? Do you need the check? Can you get the hell out of here already?!"

I understand "Are you done yet?" seems like an innocent question. There is curiosity. If we have five children now, how far will we go? I'd be curious, too, but there is a lack of boundaries in the "Are you done yet?" line of questioning. Obviously this is a sensitive subject and not really anyone else's business. People would never even ask a friend, let alone a stranger, when they plan to get their hair cut, for fear of offending, yet for some reason the "How many children are you going to have" question is fair game. This also goes for people without children. We are close with a couple who has struggled with infertility for years, and I have witnessed strangers asking how long they'd been married immediately followed by "Why don't you have any children?" Total disregard for what they might be going through. Why is this? I don't mean to get up on a diaper box, but individual liberties are all-important in this country . . . except when it comes to the number of kids you have or don't have.

Often I suspect "Are you done yet?" may mask a thinly veiled judgment against my having five children. Maybe some people think that Jeannie and I are being greedy by having five children, that there is a limited supply of babies, and we are exceeding our fair share. Maybe they think that we are inhibiting a woman's right to choose and single-handedly attacking access to birth control. We all have heard the arguments against having "too many children." What about the overpopulation problem? What about the starving children in Africa? What about your carbon footprint? I have over a hundred comedian friends who are not having children by choice. Maybe I'm having their children. I care about starvation in Africa, but I doubt the probability of our having one less child will somehow feed people. As for the carbon footprint, the seven people in my family live in a two-bedroom five-story walk-up apartment. Normally, you can't walk three steps without running into someone. We don't own a car or a pet farting cow. I can safely assume our carbon footprint is smaller than a lot of people's. I'm not saying it's smaller than *your* footprint, but then again, you did buy this book. Do you realize how many trees you killed? I've heard that for really good books like this, they use at least one tree per page. Don't worry—since it is *this* book, I forgive you. And so do the trees. You have used your carbon footprint wisely. If you were going to destroy the environment, at least you did it for me. If this is an e-book version, please feel guilty about something else.

So, no kids, one kid, five kids, or sixteen kids, I say we just live and let live. This is the land of the free and the home of the brave enough to have five kids. Judging other people says more about you than about the person you're judging. Except of course when you're judging people with too many cats. And by that, I mean more than one cat. Those people are completely bonkers and should be locked up. A good friend of ours has three cats in her studio apartment and asked me, "Can you tell that I have cats?" I replied, "No, but I can tell you have a box of turds in your living room." She recently told me that she had just gotten a new kitten. Obviously I asked her, "Are you done yet?"

Six Kids, Catholic

Big families are not new to me; I was one of six children. We were "Six kids, Catholic." I remember saying that as a teenager to people when they asked how many children were in my family. There would always be a beat after I said "Six kids," for the person to silently speculate about the size of our family; then I would give the explanation, "Catholic." Strange how that seemed to be a satisfactory answer: "Six kids, Catholic." I sometimes wondered if I didn't follow the "Six kids" with "Catholic," someone might have said, "Six kids? Wow, your mom must be a whore."

Truth be told, my parents were Catholic but it wasn't like the pope told my mom and dad how many children to have. They just liked kids. Well, my mom did, anyway. I suppose the Catholic explanation for the large family was my quick justification for the size of our family. Similar to how heavy drinkers seem to blame their drinking on their ethnic heritage. "I'm not an alcoholic, I'm Irish American."

Growing up, this is how my family dressed all the time.

I loved growing up in a big family, but everyone from a big family always says they loved growing up in a big family. It seems a little suspicious. Like when people brag about growing up in the Bronx. Nobody questions their sincerity, but have you ever been to the Bronx?

Honestly, I have nothing to compare the big family experience to. I was the youngest of six children. The scrape of the pot. My parents tried their best, but they were exhausted. It was like the last half hour of a brunch buffet. It's still a great meal, but let's just say at that point, the guy working at the omelet station has lost some of his enthusiasm. Parents burn out in big families. You can even see it in the naming of children.

Nobody told me it was black tie.

The first kid: "You were named after your grandfather." The sixth kid: "You were named after a sandwich I ate. I loved that sandwich. Now go get your brother, Reuben." My parents had had five teenagers lie to them before I even asked to borrow the car. By the time they got to me, they were beyond suspicious. They were illogical. "Can I go roller skating?" "No! We won't have you ending up pregnant like your sister."

Given that I come from "Six kids, Catholic," I shouldn't be surprised when people assume my large family is for religious reasons. I'm Catholic. Everyone knows Mormons, Catholics, and Orthodox Jews have large families. So it is for religious reasons, right? I've found that's not how it works. If anything, you have four or five kids and THEN you become religious. Believe me, once you lose a kid in a New York City park, atheist or not, you start talking to God right away. "Hey, God, I know I haven't talked to you in a while . . . probably since that last pregnancy test. I guess it's kind of ironic, me reaching out, having lost that same kid. Anyway, if you can help me find my son, I promise I will never do anything bad again. I won't even eat at Wendy's— oh, wait. There he is. Never mind, God. Well, we're off to Wendy's. Talk to you when I get cancer." Kids and disease are the true gateways to faith.

Then why so many? Friends often ask this question. Heck, I often wonder myself. While I can't think of my life without any one of my children, why so many of them? I like to think people would understand when they see I'm married to a woman as beautiful and amazing as Jeannie. Then again, if the number of our children were based on how I felt about Jeannie, we would probably give the Duggars a run for their money.

Well, why not? I guess the reasons against having more children always seem uninspiring and superficial. What exactly am I missing out on? Money? A few more hours of sleep? A more peaceful meal? More hair? These are nothing compared to what I get from these five monsters who rule my life. I believe each of my five children has made me a better man. So I figure I only need another thirty-four kids to be a pretty decent guy. Each one of them has been a pump of light into my shriveled black heart. I would trade money, sleep, or hair for a smile from one of my children in a heartbeat. Well, it depends on how much hair.

There are hidden benefits of having five kids. Besides the unconditional love, the most obvious is the free pass. When you have five kids, you are invited to far fewer social events. I know this may seem like a negative to some, but let's be serious, it's a positive. People don't invite you to stay at their houses anymore. Thank God. People are far more forgiving of social failures. "We never received a thank-you note from the Gaf-figans." "Honey, they have five kids. We are lucky they even showed up. Let's not invite them next time." Having five kids is like having a perpetual doctor's excuse.

You actually are forced to clean up and simplify your life by what is called the TMK factor: Too Many Kids. Their wedding is in Alaska? How do we get out of that? TMK. Everyone has to volunteer for the school safety patrol? Not us. TMK. People go to the gym and work out? Not me. TMK.

I sometimes wonder what explanation my children will provide for our large family. "Five kids, Catholic" would be too easy. "Five kids, Dad Crazy" would be too on the nose. "Five kids, my parents had a healthy sex life" would be too much information. I can't believe you even brought that one up! I guess I don't care how they explain it as long as they don't say, "Thirty-four kids, Catholic."

The Great White Baby

As a parent, you always secretly hope other people will find your baby as adorable and as special as you do. When our first child, Marre, was a baby I did a couple of shows in China, and Jeannie and the baby came along. Let me be clear that I have a great respect for the Chinese, and I don't just say that because we are all going to be working for them in a couple of years. During our visit, the Chinese people were very polite and warm. They seemed especially enamored with fifteen-month-old Marre, with whom we strolled all around Shanghai and Beijing. What can I say? She is that adorable. I remember thinking, "This baby is a star!" It seemed that most Chinese had never seen anything like her before. As we walked around Shanghai, people would smile and point at the superpale blue-eyed baby girl with the mop of blonde curls. It was very flattering until we got to the Great Wall.

The Great Wall of China is one of the Seven Wonders of

the World, and for good reason. The views are captivating, and, given the number of tourists from China visiting the wall, it is an obvious source of national pride. There were a handful of tourists from across the globe and large tourist groups from all over China in bright-colored windbreakers. As Jeannie and I approached the Great Wall, we were flattered when three fifty-year-old Chinese women in matching orange windbreakers wanted a picture of Marre. "You want a picture of my beautiful daughter? But of course." When we reached the Great Wall, there was another request from two teenage Chinese girls in purple windbreakers. "Well, sure." Suddenly the requests became more frequent. Eventually the Chinese tourists stopped asking and started taking pictures of Marre sitting in her stroller. At one point, my fifteen-month-old was completely encircled by a crowd of Chinese tourists in bright windbreakers, all taking pictures of her. Suddenly the crowd was huge. A wave of fear poured over me. We could no longer see our baby, and I had this image of the crowd dissipating to reveal that the baby was gone. I yelled, "Enough, enough!" Well, of course, the crowd didn't know English and must have thought I was barking, "Free pictures of the giant pale baby" or something. More colored windbreakers came over. Finally I had to push people out of the way and grab my little Marre from the Chinese paparazzi.

Of course, she was safe, and I went home that day realizing I was the proud father of the Eighth Wonder of the World. Or at least of China.

The Mousetrap

Last summer I took my family on vacation. Well, I should clarify. We went to Disney World. I had some shows in Orlando and Clearwater, so I figured I would take Jeannie and the kids to Disney. I'll be a hero. Slam-dunk.

What I forgot was that Orlando in August is roughly the same temperature as the surface of the sun, and I don't like going outside. What I also didn't realize is that going to Disney as an adult is like standing in line at the DMV. The only real difference is that at the DMV at least you leave with a driver's license.

Remember when you went on vacation as a kid and you'd think to yourself, "Why is Dad always in a bad mood?" Well, now I understand. It's amazing how much money it costs to be uncomfortable all day and listen to your children whine and complain. Yes, Disney is the "happiest place on earth" to a little kid, but it's just too much stimulation. The rides, the characters, the parade, the ice cream, and the candy every ten feet. They can't handle it. They turn into monsters. "I want . . . everything!"

Disney is not a vacation. To me the term "Disney Vacation" is equivalent to the term "Chuck E. Cheese Fine Dining." A vacation means lying poolside under a very large umbrella and people bringing you frozen drinks. I don't know how we justify calling most family trips "vacations." Where is the logic? "We've worked very hard to make our life here at home as comfortable and convenient as possible, so to reward ourselves, let's travel to somewhere we've never been and try to survive for a week." Most trips have that moment of waking up in a strange, uncomfortable bed and asking yourself, "Now how do I get coffee?" Rest assured, the coffee will be bad. And expensive. But I digress. Back to Disney.

I did figure out what makes Disney so "magical." It's because you can walk around sweating your ass off for twelve hours and *still* gain weight. "I know it's a hundred degrees out here, but these fries taste great." We eat because we want to have a good time. "This churro is cheering us up, right?" In the end, that's what most vacations are. Just you eating in a place you've never been. "Why don't we eat something, then we'll go get something to eat? Then we should see that thing we're supposed to see; they probably have a snack bar, so we can get something to eat. But after that, we definitely gotta go out and get something to eat."

We eat constantly because there is pressure to have a good time on vacation. If we are lucky, we get seven days and two of those days are spent in airport security lines. So the rest of the vacation we are under this cloud of "Hurry up and have fun before we have to pack."

If there is pressure to have fun on a vacation, at Disney it's desperation. You see it on the strained faces of parents. They all seem to have this "This was an enormous mistake" expression. I remember telling my kids, "I hope you are enjoying yourselves. It was either this or send you to college. Now hurry up and have fun, because we're never coming back here."

You try to hurry up and have fun, but there's always one thing slowing you down. The lines for the rides at Disney. I stood in line for an hour and twenty minutes in hundred-degree heat for the Dumbo ride. After a minute I realized "I'm the Dumbo. I'm actually waiting in line to see myself." I almost expected there to be a huge mirror at the end of the line with some guy just pointing at me: "DUMBO!"

Some of those Disney rides make you realize how far we've come with amusement park rides. I was on the "It's a Small World" ride, and all I could think was, "There was a time when people found this entertaining?" You could be on acid and think, "I'm not getting anything here. I think I'll go back to staring at my hand. Yes, this is much better. If only I had two of these."

To be fair, some of the Disney rides are from the 1970s, when there was no competition. It doesn't seem like that much thought went into them. "Okay, um, how about a bumper car goes into a dark room and there's a picture of Winnie-the-Pooh? People would stand in line for an hour for that, right? Well, what if we hollow out a log and throw them over a waterfall?" They must have figured, "We have their money, what are they gonna do?" I must admit my favorite ride was the air-conditioned bus back to the airport. Well worth the wait.

For parents, Disney is kind of a cruel joke. A year later, you ask a five-year-old their favorite part of Disney, and they'll say, "We went to Disney? I don't remember. Can we go again?" Sorry, they went out of business.

Disney is a perfect example of one of those things you do *just* for your children. There is no possible benefit an adult can take away from the Disney experience except feeling like a superdad in your children's eyes. Now there are adults without children who go to Disney, and they are called weirdos. Very nice people. Absolutely crazy. Even the nerdiest of nerds at Comic-Con think those people are nut jobs. "Hey, I may be wearing a Batman suit, but you're waiting in line for an autograph from Aladdin? Get some perspective, dude!" I know that sounds mean, but when you are trying to entertain your kids while you wait for two hours in the boiling heat because there are four fifty-year-olds in line in front of you for Peter Pan, you'd be a little irritated, too.

Picture This

Recently I ordered school photos of my six-year-old. Now I will only have roughly three hundred thousand photos of him for this year. I have more photos of my children than times my father ever looked at me. It's almost as if I'm gathering evidence for a future trial of whether or not I was a good father. "Your Honor, as proof of the defendant's innocence, I'd like to submit 1.5 million photos that my client took of the plaintiff." As parents, we can't stop taking pictures of our kids. "Hey, take a picture of that. We'll never look at it." We take pictures of everyday life and act like we are capturing history. "Unbelievable! The cat is asleep." Click. I've calculated that if I showed you all the pictures I have of just my six-year-old, it would take roughly six years. It kind of defeats the point, right?

I suppose this happens because we have cameras on our phones. Do we need that? It's not like ten years ago we were thinking, "I wish I could take a low-quality photo of my dessert and text it to someone who's not interested."

Remember when photos were special? It was not that long ago. "It's school picture day! We better get Junior a haircut. We want him to look nice. Don't want to waste the time of that camera expert and that precious *film*." If you were one of the younger kids in your family, pictures were even *more* rare. As the youngest of six, the neighbors probably had more photos of me than my own parents did. If someone came up to me today and showed me a picture of myself when I was ten, it would be unbelievably exciting news. "You have a picture of *me* when I was *ten*? Did an archaeologist dig it out of the rubble?"

I won "Largest Head" that year.

Now we show our phone photos, apologizing, "I don't have any recent photos of my kid. This is from like a month ago. He looks totally different now." Because of cell phone cameras we have way more photos than we will ever need. What are we supposed to do with all these photos of our kids? Yes, there is the benefit of our computers running really slow, clogged with thousands of photos of the same pose, but outside of that, it's pointless. Yet we keep taking pictures. *Click, click, click.* We download all of them. We don't even weed out the bad ones. "Eh, I'll just get another computer. This will be my Disney trip computer." My parents had boxes of photos in their closets. Now we have old computers in our closets. "Hey, honey, there's our wedding computer." "There's my computer from when I was single. I guess I should destroy that one."

Snow Job

Last winter Jeannie and I took our then seven-year-old, five-year-old, two-year-old, and six-month-old skiing on the other side of the country. That seems like a good idea, right? Well, it did to this genius. I even had four months to not realize it was a ridiculous idea. No, I wasn't in a coma during that period. I spent that time busy, unaware, and planning the trip.

Our story starts in October. I had just booked some theater shows in Salt Lake City during January's Martin Luther King holiday weekend. Suddenly I had a brilliant thought: I'll bring the whole family and take my kids skiing in Park City. Perfect. It will be fun for everyone. The snow. The hot chocolate! I'll get my city kids out on the slopes. They'll love it. Sure, it might seem a little strange to have such a large family in the heart of Mormon country, but let's do it. What better way to commemorate Martin Luther King Jr. than going skiing around a bunch of rich white people?

My life feels like skiing uphill.

I actually thought I was being smart. I'm not really a skier, but I wanted to expose my young children to skiing. Friends had always talked about the joy of taking their kids skiing. Let's do this! Since I'm no ski expert, I'll make this as easy as possible. I decided we would stay at a nice ski resort. It will be expensive, but it will be worth it. Of course, I'll have to fly all the kids across the country to Salt Lake City, which is also pretty costly, but this will be *the* family vacation. I guess a six-month-old can't ski so we'll have to bring a babysitter. Okay, so that's another expense. Obviously I'm not going to buy skis or ski pants—we'll rent them. That will add an expense, but this is not just *the* family vacation, this will be *the* THE family vacation. If only cost turned out to be my only problem.

Unfortunately, I only realized this was a really bad idea when we were on the plane flying to Salt Lake. Whenever I travel with my young children, I'm always reminded of an important travel lesson: Never travel with my young children. The flight from New York to Salt Lake City is five hours, but with four young kids, it only feels like fifty. It wasn't just torture for me. Let's just say traveling across the country with a seven-year-old, five-year-old, two-year-old, and six-month-old is not really how you make friends on a plane. Pretending you don't know your kids is not funny to the businessman trying to sleep in the window seat. Apple has yet to develop a device that can engage a two-year-old. After four hours of convincing her that she could only hear the movie on the iPad with the headphones on, I became painfully aware that I'd made an enormous mistake. As the plane landed in Salt Lake, I remembered that the friends who took their kids skiing were incredibly rich. Oh, and their kids were teenagers, and their kids are only one kid, and they own a ski condo in Vermont, and I'm an idiot.

As we gathered our bags in Salt Lake, I resigned myself to the realities. I'm a fool, I can't afford this trip, and this is going to be really hard with a baby. Anyway, we were there, and I was determined to make it work. Let's enjoy it. Just a few more steps before we get to the hotel and I can start preparing for my show that night.

After the hour drive from the airport to the resort, we were advised by the lady behind the desk to go into town to pick up our skis and avoid dealing with the chaos the next morning. (I learned later there was a courtesy service included by the hotel that came to your room and fitted everyone for skis, but somehow the person checking us in had never heard of this service. They only worked at the hotel that provided the service.) After the unnecessary journey into the heart of town, renting the skis became a journey in itself. Let me be honest, most people in the world are more patient than me, and none of these people are my children. Getting your kids fitted for skis and then not taking them skiing is not fun for anybody. In defense of my children's bad behavior following a long day of traveling, we were also taking them shopping and not buying them anything.

The next day was the first day of skiing. Getting little kids dressed for skiing is not easy and may take a while, but at least by the time you finish zipping them all up, they have to go to the bathroom. For the life of me I can't figure out how I ever thought it was a good idea to take a two-year-old that has just mastered walking to a ski lesson. Eventually we got everyone to his or her ski classes, and Jeannie and I skied for ten minutes before we had to pick them up.

Katie after her $150, twenty-minute ski lesson.

After an overpriced lunch, we dropped our two-year-old off for a nap, and we went skiing as a family. Kind of. I suppose there are many approaches to skiing. Jeannie and our seven-year-old, Marre, took a more cautious, leisurely approach to the mountain. Jeannie made it clear that because she had a six-month-old and a two-year-old back at the hotel, she was not interested in doing any daredevil stuff. The approach of our five-year-old, Jack, can only be described as "straight down until you crash." There are people on *Jackass* who would find this approach reckless. I can't believe that I thought this would be relaxing at all. Even riding a chairlift with little kids who love to scare the hell out of their parents is incredibly stressful.

For some reason, ski mountains are marked with some sort of Lucky Charm marshmallow identification system. There were blue diamonds, green moons. Oh, I don't remember exactly. I just remember sticking to the green and avoiding the dreaded black diamonds. Near the end of the second and final day of skiing, everyone got more adventurous, and we were ready to move onto the blue. Well, the kids and I were. Jeannie was hesitant. She didn't want the slightest injury to interfere with the daunting task of flying back to the East Coast with the babies. At the end of the day, with some coaxing, I got Jeannie to go down one of the more difficult blue hills with the big kids and me. After reassuring her it was totally doable and fun, we dared the chairlift up.

Getting off the chairlift, our five-year-old instantaneously transformed himself into a bullet, went barreling down the hill, and immediately wiped out. I skied down and helped him up. I then helped my seven-year-old up. Then helped my five-year-old up again. Then helped my seven-year-old up again. Then they both helped me up. After a long string of killer wipeouts, eventually we made it down the hill. At the bottom, we waited for Jeannie. Then we waited some more. My children asked, "Where's Momma?" I giggled, thinking how mad Jeannie would be at me for having her do the more difficult hill. After way too long of staring up at the hill and waiting for Jeannie, they began to close the ski lifts, signaling the end of the day. Starting to panic, I asked ski patrol for assistance. I was assured they wouldn't leave anyone on the mountain. Wouldn't leave anyone on the mountain? What? The kids became more concerned, and I tried to be cool. Then another half hour passed as I watched the ski patrol making plans for what they would do that night. Okay. Now I was frightened. I began to consider the reality that my wife had skied off a cliff and died, leaving me with four young children all because I dragged her across the country to go skiing. I had also convinced her to ski a hill she didn't want to take. I was not only the worst father in the world, I think I could be prosecuted for murder.

After about an hour of bargaining with God, the ski patrol central got a radio call that a woman on the slopes had been hit from behind by a snowboarder. It was Jeannie! She had accidentally ended up on one of the dreaded black diamond hills. Apparently her "optional" helmet saved her life. She had been recovering in some sort of ski patrol station and was skiing back down, shaken up but not injured. I began to breathe again and put on my stoic daddy face as I dried my kids' tears and told them Mommy was okay. Luckily, Jeannie was too relieved to be mad at me.

When we finally arrived back in New York City and settled into our cramped apartment, I did a head count. We were all alive. A little poorer, but alive. All in all, the ski trip was worth it. We can go a year without groceries, but I can't go a day without a wife.

On the Road Again

During summer and spring vacations, I take my kids camping. Well, actually I take my kids on a giant tour bus so Jeannie and I can work and the kids can pretend they are camping.

I wish I liked camping. Then again, I also wish I liked running marathons and eating vegetables. I know my children would love to camp, and I'm also sure my children would love a dog, but given the size of our apartment and the fact that Jeannie is supposedly allergic, that's not going to happen either. I think she's just allergic to the fact she would be the only one taking care of the dog.

I guess you could say I'm allergic to camping. Jeannie loves camping because she says camping was a tradition in her family. I always point out that prior to the invention of the house, camping was a tradition in everyone's family. I don't get camping. "Hey, want to burn a couple of vacation days sleeping on the ground outside? Chances are you'll wake up freezing and covered in a rash?" No, thanks. If camping is so great, why are the bugs always trying to get in your house? My parents never took me camping, and I think it was because they loved me. Has anyone ever been a happy camper? Whenever we use that term "happy camper," we're being sarcastic. "He is NOT a happy camper." Why don't we just call the person a camper? He's miserable. You know who's a happy camper? The guy leaving the campsite. He gets to take a shower. I've tried to explain to my children that we do a different type of camping that includes a tour bus, hotels, and best of all, no camping.

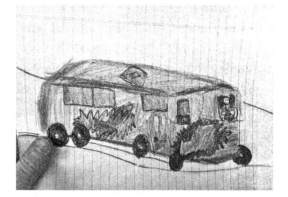

So why a tour bus? Although I complain about my children, I really do hate being away from them. I learned quickly that being gone for a weekend doing shows can easily turn into being gone for a week doing shows. Our initial solution was to bring our children for long weekends whenever we could. As our clan grew, this quickly became cost-prohibitive. Our solution was a tour bus.

Yes, a tour bus. People often think we mean a Winnebago or a large van but we're talking about an actual tour bus like rock stars use, but there's no stripper pole. This may seem like overkill, but it makes perfect sense. The bus is roughly the same size as our apartment but it gets better. The tour bus means no airports. No security lines. No taking little kids through security lines at airports. Our bus picks us up at our apartment building, we load everyone and all the stuff on, and we are off doing shows. The bus is expensive to rent, so we do a show a night as we dart across North America for usually two weeks. Some kids go to Florida or a have a summerhouse. Our children will have "bus camping" memories.

There are six bunks and a large bed on the tour bus. Perfect for me, Jeannie, our five children, and a babysitter who always seems to quit whenever we get back from our camping bus tour. We also bring a portable crib or "travel cage." We drive mostly at night because children don't really understand the concept of "no walking" while the bus is moving.

On a typical day, we wake up on the bus in a new city and head into a hotel to check in. We don't really need the hotel because we have the bus, but we need the hotel pool and the

Happy Camper

breakfast. They are usually nonfancy hotels that provide a "complimentary" breakfast. I should point out that this "complimentary" breakfast is neither complimentary of the hotel or of the meal of breakfast. We are always grateful to have it, but it often feels like a breakfast garage sale.

> HOTEL MANAGER: Okay, corporate headquarters says we have to offer a free breakfast, but they won't give us any money.
>
> EMPLOYEE #1: Well, we could make some biscuits and gravy from papier-mâché?
>
> EMPLOYEE #2: I heard a middle school went out of business—maybe we could get their juice machine. It's from the 1950s, but who cares?
>
> HOTEL MANAGER: Great ideas. All right, moving on. How much can we overcharge for Internet access?

We loved the ducks at the Peabody Hotel. They were delicious!

After breakfast, we try to see a local tourist attraction. I've taken my children to parks, fairs, and zoos all across the U.S. and Canada. I've taken my children to see Mount Rushmore. It wasn't a big decision. We were in Rapid City, and it really came down to either seeing Mount Rushmore or doing nothing. Mount Rushmore is beautiful, even though my children were disappointed at the absence of rides. "Is that a slide?" "No, that's Thomas Jefferson's nose." The Black Hills of South Dakota are breathtaking. They are sacred to the Lakota Indians, and out of respect, our government had someone carve four white guys' faces into one of their mountains.

LAKOTA INDIAN: These hills are sacred to us.
CARVER: [*Chiseling.*] Yeah, yeah. I'll be done in a couple of decades. These guys I'm carving were all about freedom. Especially the two who owned slaves.

After seeing a local sight, we usually head to the hotel pool. Every hotel we stay at must have a pool. For us, staying at a hotel with a pool is probably more important than staying at a hotel with beds. The hotel pools are really my kids' favorite part of our bus trips. This is because young children love any kind of pool. Indoor, outdoor, aboveground, cesspool, it doesn't matter. They may hate taking a bath, but they love a pool. It could be March, and a pool could be freezing, covered in leaves and bugs, and one of my children will beg, "Daddy, can we go in? Oh, please? Please!" I always tell them to ask their mother to put on her swimsuit.

You can usually tell a hotel has an indoor pool because the

Whole family at Mt. Rushmore.
Our babysitter quit the day we got back to NYC.

lobby will smell like a bucket of bleach. I'm always tempted to
ask someone at the front desk, "Do you have an indoor pool,
or did someone just clean up a murder scene? 'Cause my eyes
are bleeding." Swimming with my kids is really fun. It's not
really great for the unlucky business traveler at the pool who
wanted to have a relaxing swim. When we have our five kids in
the hotel pool, strangers always look at us like we are overzealous dog walkers. On more than one occasion, I've witnessed a
business traveler enter the hotel swimming pool area, see our
screaming, swimming children, and immediately turn around
and walk out. They probably think there really is no difference

between swimming in a pool with five little kids and swimming in a toilet. Swimming is really the first time a little kid can multitask. "I can play AND pee? This is amazing." Let it be known I have no proof that any of my kids have peed in a pool, but other kids with worse parents probably do.

For some reason the water is much warmer in this area.

After my children have ruined the pool, we all head back to the soon-to-be-ruined hotel room. I'll head to the bus to get ready for that night's show. Jeannie and the babysitter will bathe and feed the kids before putting them to sleep on the bus. Jeannie will then meet me at the show. I'll do the show, and then Jeannie and I will head back to the bus to depart.

Why are we putting the kids to bed on the bus when we have a hotel room that we've already paid for? Actually in order to make these trips work, we often pay for two nights at a hotel and don't sleep at that hotel. When you are driving overnight and arrive at a hotel at 8 a.m., you can't check in until at least 3 p.m. So we have to pay for the hotel room the night before. To make matters more interesting, the hotel room that we've paid for the night before at which we've arrived at 8 a.m. requires that we check out at 3 p.m. But we have a show that night at 8 p.m., and at 11 p.m., we leave that city on the bus to get to the next city. Therefore, even though we are still not sleeping overnight at the hotel after the show, we must also pay for *that* night at the hotel. And that's how you pay for two nights at a hotel and never sleep there. This word problem will continue until I can figure out a way to get a tour bus with a pool.

So after the show, we leave the hotel parking lot and drive off to the next campsite. A campsite without a tent, a fire, or bug spray. My favorite kind of campsite. One with Internet access and a shower.

Eskimo Pies

Every night before I get my one hour of sleep, I have the same thought: "Well, that's a wrap on another day of acting like I know what I'm doing." I wish I were exaggerating, but I'm not. Most of the time, I feel entirely unqualified to be a parent. I call these times being awake. I really do try to be a good dad. I mean "try," because nothing about parenting has come naturally to me. Last summer, we had four children, and I noticed there were only three Eskimo pies left in the freezer for dessert. The first thought that came to me was, "Well, looks like I'm eating three Eskimo pies." In spite of my lack of parental instincts, in the end I did the right thing. I only ate one. That way the four of them could split the last two evenly. How else are they going to learn math? Just trying to do my part.

There is no training camp for being a parent. No special school and no daddy doctorate degree. I try to learn by observing other people, but parenting just seems to come easier for them. My wife is no exception.

Jeannie makes parenting look so easy. Observing her mother our children is like watching rhythmic gymnastics. So smooth, so energetic, so smiley. I think mothers have an unfair advantage. They've had a nine-month head start on the bonding thing. The baby already knows the mother's voice, heartbeat, and tempo. Of course, the baby will automatically like her better. It's favoritism, really. Sure, men are encouraged to bond during pregnancy, but it always feels a little esoteric to me. Men are told to talk to the baby in utero via the mother's lower abdomen. That's not awkward at all. Especially when your six-year-old walks in with his friend. "Uh, why is your dad doing that?"

I feel like nature also cheated me in the nurturing department. I don't even have breasts. Well, I kind of do, but not the kind a newborn or anyone else is interested in. Nurturing for a mother is instinctive. While breastfeeding, the mother is not just feeding the baby, she is nurturing the baby. From that time on, everything the mother does seems to have that added element of natural nurture. Meals, stories, laundry, and organizing their rooms have this nurturing element. They are not just doing "chores." It is a natural instinct for the mother to make the child feel safe, protected, and comfortable. She is driven to do these things and actually *wants* to do these things. I can kind of relate because I have really strong natural instincts to eat cheese and take naps.

I think most men have to be instructed how to nurture a newborn. When our first child was born, I actually googled "Men bonding with a newborn." I need instruction. Most men need to follow directions. That's why men love the GPS system. It's no mistake that the GPS voice is female. Men could really use a "Daddy GPS."

GPS VOICE: In one-tenth of a minute, your toddler will bump his head on the coffee table. Prepare to show sympathy and caring . . . Recalculating!

Before you think this is a diatribe about the differences between men and women, I confess that it's not just my gender that contributes to my ineptitude as a parent. I wish it was that easy to explain away. A lot of men have nurturing instincts that you don't need breasts for, and they take shape by doing manly things with your kids. I can't even relate to this. I am totally intimidated by other dads. I actually feel as though I'm missing some of the man genes. I don't have a workbench or a toolbox. Hell, Home Depot commercials make me feel like a sissy. I don't care about golf or cars. If I weren't obsessed with football and steak I probably would have to turn in my testicles. I'll never be inviting my son down to my woodshop so we can handcraft a go-cart together. Don't they sell those things at Target, anyway? They probably deliver, too.

It's not just in comparison to moms or other dads that I feel inferior; it's to all other parents in general. To me, it seems like other parents are smarter, more organized, and more patient. Other parents remember that the napkin is as important an element to the ice-cream cone as the ice cream and the cone. Maybe even more important. Other parents remember to bring drinks to the park and towels to the beach. Not me. "Today we are going to let the sun dry you off. If you're thirsty, head over to the water fountain the homeless guy is sleeping under." Other parents seem calmer and filled with endless patience. I watch them in awe at the park. "Hunter, Mommy is not pleased with your behavior right now." I always have to hold myself back from yelling at other people's bratty kids, "Shut up, Hunter, or I'll come over to your house and break all your toys! What kind of name is Hunter anyway? Good luck with that." By the way, never try to discipline another parent's kid unless you are a teacher or a lifeguard. You will only come off like a lunatic. Well, at least that's what a friend told me.

I do have moments of hope. Just when I am positive that I am the least qualified parent out there, I will witness one of my calm friends with kids lose it and yell at their kids. I feel like I've won the lottery. Truth is, all parents snap. I'm sure even Deepak Chopra snapped at his kids. Seeing a friend raise their voice at their child should make me cringe, but it always gives me an enormous sense of relief.

I do try my best. All fathers do. Well, most of them do. Well, most don't. But, let's face it, the task is overwhelming. This is why most fathers have ridiculous hobbies like golf and ice fishing. Why would someone volunteer to wake up early on their day off to hit a tiny ball around a field while roasting in the hot sun or to sit on a frozen pond in the middle of winter unless it was easier than being an involved dad? I will always feel inadequate in comparison to the natural instincts of a mother, so it is much easier to do the manly thing and run away. Since I am anti-outdoors, when I run away, I watch football. I relate to the quarterback. Most of my life feels like I'm down a touchdown with forty-eight seconds left in the game. The odds are against me, but I still have to *try*, right?

You're Going to Miss This

It seemed only yesterday Jeannie was having a baby. Of course, it *was* yesterday that Jeannie was having a baby, but what I'm saying is that they grow up fast. When I'm with all my little ones, people with grown or teenage children always tell me, "You're going to miss this." I have to assume they are talking about my children being young and not the conversation I'm having with them, because I am not going to miss people giving me advice about children.

From the moment the baby bump shows, strangers view it as an open invitation to give unsolicited advice about everything baby related: "Your wife shouldn't be walking up stairs!" "Looks like your wife is having a boy." Then, with the newborn: "Isn't your baby hot?" "Isn't your baby cold?" Or my favorite regarding the baby in a sling: "Can he breathe in there?" No, he can't. And I plan to put you in here next.

Of course "You're going to miss this" is not typical advice.

It's a confession from these parents with older children that they may have not taken enough time to appreciate the chaos. It is a sincere, generous confession. That's why when people tell me, "You are going to miss this," I always offer to let them take a trip down memory lane and come over and change some of Patrick's diapers at 4 a.m. or tell my three-year-old the same Scooby-Doo story for five hours.

I get it. Well, I think I do. I know I will miss how small and cute my children are. I already miss how much lighter they were to carry to bed last month. I'll miss my kids' sincere excitement at wanting to see their daddy. Our fifteen-month-old, Michael, thinks I'm the greatest person on this planet. Granted, he's only known me for fifteen months.

I'll miss lying to them and actually getting away with it. I'll miss being smarter than they is. I'll miss the confiscated candy bowl in the cupboard. I'll miss the access to kid food. Did you know you can't go into Chuck E. Cheese's without a kid? Where else except everywhere am I going to get horrible pizza?

I'll miss being embarrassed by their behavior in places like grocery stores—"Don't eat that!" Especially when they are eventually embarrassed by *my* behavior in grocery stores— "Dad, don't eat that!" I suppose it's ironic, after all the public toddler meltdowns, that my children will someday be embarrassed by me. I know it's going to happen. I know every parent has to deal with it. Maybe even God had to deal with this:

JESUS: Dad, just drop me off at that manger and pick me up around Easter.

Of course, I don't think I'm God, but I am a little godlike to my children. This is what I'm going to miss the most. Even though they don't view me as the tyrant I'd hope to be, to them I'm all-powerful: I'm their creator and provider. They love me and kind of fear me. They want to be in my arms when they are scared. They want my forgiveness after they've done something wrong—"Daddy, are you happy at me?" They want to be with me. I know this won't last. The expectations have been set too high. It's only a matter of time before they are totally disappointed when I fall off that lofty pedestal and they realize I'm just a giant kid myself. It's at that point I'll run into some dad with a toddler gazing up at him in wonder, and I'll say, "You're going to miss this." And he'll say, "Hey, aren't you the Hot Pocket guy?"

Additional Acknowledgments

Oh, good, you're reading the additional acknowledgments. It's important for me to thank the people who helped me give birth to this book. To me, for some reason, most acknowledgments in books read a little bit like a bland acceptance speech. "I'd like to thank my editor and other people with names." I can always hear the author saying "Yeah, I wrote the book, and this other guy negotiated my deal, and this lady did something else." This is not the case with *Dad Is Fat*.

Sometimes acknowledgment pages feel like an opportunity for the author to name-drop. Me and my dear friends Bono and Bishop Tutu always complain about people who do that.

I'd like to thank my manager, Alex Murray, and my book agent, Simon Green, who patiently waited two years for me to finally figure out what type of book I wanted to write about being a father. I'd also like to thank my editor, Suzanne O'Neill, her assistant Anna Thompson, and the gang at Crown Archetype, like Tina Constable, Mauro DiPreta, Meredith McGinnis, Tammy Blake, and Tommy Cabrera, who personally mailed three thousand autographed bookplates that looked amazingly similar to a "Hello My Name Is . . ." name tag.

Thanks to the many photographers who provided some of the great pictures, including Mindy Tucker, Kai Cheung, Corey Melton, and, of course, Monsignor Donald Sakano of St. Patrick's Basilica.

Thanks to my children's great babysitters and teachers, who helped us take care of our most precious possessions while we worked on the book, and to all of the great schools, Nazareth Nursery, Little Missionary, WCLA, Avenues, and Marymount, for being so understanding when we fogot to pick up a kid.

Many friends (Tom Shillue, Karen Bergreen, and Rob Hubbs) and family members (Felicia Noth, Dom Noth, and Joe Gaffigan) helped with insight and encouragement. I must also thank the other "Cincos" (parents of five children) in my life: Trey and Nora Fitzpatrick and Mitch and Chris Gaffigan, who provided invaluable insight about the impossible task of raising a basketball team; and Mike and Tracy Murphy, who made it look so damn easy. Of course, I need to thank Joe Jackson, the father of the Jackson 5, for proving you can look good being the father of five. Okay, the Jacksons had six kids. There was Janet. Wait, there was also La Toya. Forget Joe Jackson.

Jim Gaffigan is a comedian, actor, writer, and former grocery store stock boy from Indiana. Mr. Gaffigan lived by himself for over thirteen years. He presently lives in a small two-bedroom apartment in New York City with his five young children and his more talented, much better-looking, and very fertile wife, Jeannie.

© Corey Melton